Praise for

The Seven Levels of Communication

"The ability to build relationships is the backbone of a successful business. The phone call, the handshake, the lunch meeting—that's where business is done, and Michael Maher knows how to do it. If you want to win in business, you've got to learn how to win with people, and this book will show you how to do just that."

> **Dave Ramsey**, Host of The Dave Ramsey Show and NY Times Bestselling Author of *The Total Money Makeover*

"(7L) is the clearest, most concise book I've read on what it takes to be a great salesperson. It is obvious why Michael J. Maher is one of the greatest sales people in the world. (7L) will become a classic and I plan to use it in our training."

> **Larry Kendall**, Author of *Ninja Selling*

"Master the generosity game and you can build a powerful, referral-based business. The good news is that anyone can do it! Put the wisdom of this book into practice and you can succeed at a higher level."

> **Gary Keller**, Co-Founder and Chairman of the Board, Keller Williams Realty International and *New York Times* Bestselling Author of *The Millionaire Real Estate Agent, The Millionaire Real Estate Investor* and *SHIFT: How Top Real Estate Agents Tackle Tough Times*

"Every real estate agent needs to read this book and give it to all their referral partners! In (7L), Michael Maher shows you how to build a recession-proof network that will continue to send you business no matter what the market conditions."

> **Dr. Ivan Misner**, *New York Times* Bestselling Author of *Masters of Sales* and Founder of BNI and Referral Institute

"(7L) is the most reliable and sensible business building system I have ever seen . . . If you follow this amazingly simple recipe, I guarantee success will follow you."

Todd Duncan, *New York Times* Bestselling Author of *Time Traps* and *High Trust Selling*

"It's easy to focus on what we say rather than how we say it. Maher's book will teach you how to communicate in a way that literally turns your relationships into referrals—most of the time without you even having to ask."

Tom Hopkins, Sales Trainer and Bestselling Author of *How to Master the Art of Selling* and *How to Master the Art of Listing and Selling Real Estate*

"Ready to stop wasting money on advertising? Learn from the man who built a world-class business by investing in relationships. It's warm . . . it's effective. Michael Maher has shown that building a referral generating community is not only a nicer way of doing business, but a superior business model that can work for you."

Howard Brinton, Founder and Former CEO of Star Power Systems, Hall of Fame Speaker (RE/MAX, CRS)

"Think your market is down? Maybe it's you! Michael Maher—one of the best innovators and professionals of the 21st Century—will show you how to recognize and adjust to today's market and build a business that can weather any recession! Read (7L) now."

Allan Domb, Star Power Star and commonly known as North America's Top-Producing Real Estate Agent

"Michael Maher explains that there are certain levels of communication that offer a very high return on your investment. With that in mind, I can't think of a better investment than this book."

Floyd Wickman, Founder of Sweathogs, Bestselling Author of six books, NSA Hall of Fame Sales Trainer, one of REALTOR® Magazine's 25 Most Influential People in Real Estate

"The Preeminent Productivity GPS for All Real Estate Sales Professionals! Implement the (7L) Plan immediately!"

"Michael Maher's (7L) *The Seven Levels of Communication* is a must read for the serious real estate pro. He knows what it takes to deliver five-star customer service from the heart with commitment and generosity."

"(7L) *The Seven Levels of Communication* is a terrific book. A proven, no-fail formula for success in real estate sales (though, these principles would work in any type of sales) from one of the most successful real estate professionals in modern times. Rarely have I read a book that teaches so powerfully while keeping the reader so involved. This book—written in the form of a fictional story—is a gem that will help anyone who follows its instruction touch a lot more lives and make a lot more money in the process. If you run a sales organization, consider promoting this book to everyone on your team. If you are beginning in sales or even a long-time veteran of the sales profession, invest in this book for yourself. You'll be glad you did."

"A true relationship is a treasured gift. Michael Maher shows us the path to building a relationship and the value each and every one has not just to our businesses but to us as people."

"There are few people that I consider a master at the referral business and Michael Maher is at the head of his class. This compelling story weaves a tale of how to create a network of people that is so powerful yet so simple to implement. By simply following and implementing the concepts in (7L) *The Seven Levels of Communication*, your foundation for a successful career in sales will be automatic. So set aside the time for some serious, yet fun reading!"

> **Bob Corcoran**, Founder of Corcoran Consulting & Coaching, Author of *Make a Commitment: Soar to Success in Real Estate*

"In (7L), Maher does a great job in showing how to leverage technology but not be consumed by it. He states in Chapter 8 that our online interaction is a "promise"—the promise of a future interaction whether via phone or in person. I believe many sales and relationships fail because at times we can rely too heavily on social media and emails. Maher provides tools, ideas and more importantly the concepts of how to do business the right way."

> **James Nellis**, #11 in RE/MAX USA (2009), Certified CRS Instructor and Star Power Star

"There are very few books where the reader learns, is inspired and, at the same time, enjoys the reading experience. That is precisely what Michael Maher has accomplished with his (7L) *The Seven Levels of Communication: Go from Relationships to Referrals*. This easy read takes you on a journey of proven strategies to increase your business success and you'll find it rewarding to know that nice guys/gals can finish first!"

> **Rick DeLuca**, Rick DeLuca Seminars, internationally-renowned Real Estate Trainer

"Michael has mastered the art of relationships, and in (7L) he truly inspires us all to take our businesses to the next level."

> **Brad Korn**, Owner of Cyberstars, Star Power Star, and Top-Producing Real Estate Agent

THE SEVEN LEVELS
OF COMMUNICATION

GO FROM RELATIONSHIPS TO REFERRALS

MICHAEL J. MAHER

BENBELLA BOOKS, INC.

Dallas, Texas

BenBella Books, Inc.
10440 N. Central Expressway
Suite #800
Dallas, TX 75231
www.benbellabooks.com
Send feedback to feedback@benbellabooks.com

Printed in the United States of America
10 9 8 7 6 5
ISBN-13: 978-1-942952-47-3

The Library of Congress has catalogued the hardcover edition as follows:
Michael J. (Realtor)
    (7L) : the seven levels of communication / Michael J. Maher.
        pages cm
ISBN 978-1-940363-21-9 (trade cloth)
    1. Business referrals. 2. Customer relations. 3. Success in business.
4. Real estate agents—Psychology. I. Title.
    HF5438.25.M3243 2014
    658.4'5—dc23

                                                        2013044611

Text composition by John Reinhardt Book Design
Printed by Lake Book Manufacturing

Distributed to the trade by Two Rivers Distribution, an Ingram Brand
www.tworiversdistribution.com

DEDICATION

To my father, Patrick Joseph Maher. He was a high school teacher and coach who taught me and many others until his death at the age of 54 after a three-year battle with cancer. During those three years, I learned more about my dad than I had in the nearly 20 years before. One of his regrets was not writing his memoirs—and what words of wisdom those would have been! You will not only be learning from me during your time with this book, but you will also be learning from my father. He passed away on September 1, 1992 and had over 1000 people at his funeral.

Dad, we wrote this together.

CONTENTS

INTRODUCTION

I HEARD MY HEART FLAT-LINE. The heartbeat monitor screamed its alarm.

Soon after, I opened my eyes to a large German woman all in white hovering over me. Heaven? No, Heaven wasn't quite ready for me yet.

"Welcome back. You gave us quite a scare there," said the head nurse.

I wasn't even thinking I was dying. Not me. It was too unbelievable. It wasn't my time. It couldn't be. I was in good health. I looked around the hospital room and I realized . . . I almost DIED just now. Reality hit me. Tears welled up in my eyes. I fear very little, but I was scared. I am NOT a crier, but as they prepped me for surgery to implant a temporary pacemaker, I was frightened to tears.

I remember looking at the nurse's chalkboard in the room on which December 18, 2007 was written. I thought, "I can't die on that date. There is nothing significant about December 18, 2007." Then I thought of my wife, Sheri. She would kill me if I died! She does not take loss well and I knew she would be mad as well as sad. The cardiologist asked me her name and number. I told him quietly and asked him to hold off on calling her. I would have to coach him on how to approach her.

Another thought flashed through my mind. I don't have any children. Sheri and I had discussed children, but never seriously. I was ambivalent to the idea—until that moment. I now wanted a child.

Something else came to mind and frankly, it surprised me a little. I thought of my father. My father was a high school teacher. He was very influential in the community and coached three sports. With that schedule, he was busy. When we talked, it was mostly about sports . . . until he got cancer. During a poignant moment just before his death, he shared with me his only regret; he had not written his memoirs. Thinking about him and his words that day made me realize I had knowledge, a system, and a belief that needed to be shared. This book, the one you have in your hands or on your screen at this moment, is the accumulation of my learning, implementing, failing, and evaluating the strategies necessary to build a business based on others recommending me and my services. In your hands, you hold the strategies, techniques, and systems I used—and continue to use daily—to become known as *"America's Most Referred Real Estate Professional."*

As I have been blessed with greater success, I have had the privilege of teaching and coaching others to do the same. This book tells the story of many of my coaching clients and members of my team; men and women who are ready to evolve from the Ego Era to the Generosity Generation. They are ready to stop wasting money on costly personal promotion and invest in relationships. They want to build more than a business; they want to leave a legacy.

If you want a business that will outlive you, this book will show you how to build it. If you are ready to build a large, highly profitable business using nothing but word of mouth, this book will provide you with the strategies, techniques, and resources you need. It is my hope that it will lead you not only to greater financial freedom, but also to a more fulfilling existence.

I wish my dad had put together his memoirs. It would be such a great read. I am now the father of a precious little boy. I imagine sitting on the floor during reading time with Max and reading my dad's stories, advice, and wisdom. After reading this book again, I realize that my dad and I wrote this together. I am honoring his legacy by passing on this knowledge. I survived that fateful day to help, teach, and coach others.

What had almost killed me? It turned out to be blood clots—a complication from knee surgery I had four days prior. There is a Friedrich Nietzsche quote, *"What doesn't kill us only makes us stronger."* Here's my advice to let you know you don't have to nearly die to truly live:

"Don't wait for a life-changing event to change your life."

Showing is better than telling.

What you are about to immerse yourself into is a story that is loaded with actionable content. Though all characters, scenes, and scenarios are fictional and any references to real people or actual events are unintended, all lessons, results, and testimonials are based on the true accounts and experiences of top-producing salespeople, coaching clients, and the author. Using Maher's "Power Parable" format, the author has the ability to not only tell you the strategies and tactics, like in a typical non-fiction book, but also *show* you Rick's implementation, and resulting transformation.

I hope you enjoy the story. I wrote it for you.

LUNCH OF A LIFETIME

"*R*ICK, TO BE HONEST WITH YOU, *I don't think you'll be in the business a year from now."*

The words rang in Rick's ears as the alarm jolted him out of an uneasy slumber. Two weeks had passed and he still couldn't get the image of that smirking, self-satisfied face out of his mind. With less than an hour until his lunch appointment and his bed feeling more comfortable than ever, he briefly debated canceling; after all, it was just another lender . . .

No, he thought, he'd better go. A free meal was a free meal, and he needed to get up anyway.

Rick stepped over yesterday's clothes and fumbled around the bathroom for his shaving cream. Thirty minutes later, he had showered and was driving his beloved BMW, the last of his souvenirs from the good old glory days. He indulged in a momentary flashback of how he had bought it with cash he made from just two months of commissions. Pulling onto the highway, he thought sullenly, *those were the days.*

He looked up to check the exit number, and as if to add insult to injury, he caught a glimpse of Don Dasick's new billboard. There it was: the smirking, cap-toothed smile, slicked-back hair, and a caption that read "Dial Don!" Rick cringed involuntarily. *Well, the old guy must be doing something right. He's still selling more than the rest of us in the office put together.*

It was 11:27 A.M. when Rick shuffled into EVT Restaurant for his 11:30 lunch appointment. He felt his stomach rumble, but his hunger was overshadowed by his need for coffee. The dining room was already humming with quiet conversation punctuated by the clinking of glasses, silver and fine china. Rick glanced around him. He had seen the place numerous times—the building towered over the highway he took home from work—but this was his first look inside.

The huge marble columns in the atrium drew his eyes up from the walnut wood of the hostess stand to the magnificent chandeliers dangling from the ceiling, which must have been at least forty feet high. Comfortable booths lined the walls, giving the place a luxurious and elegant appearance while maintaining a cozy feeling at the same time. How come he had never been here before?

"Katherine!"

The woman's delighted voice interrupted the subdued buzz of the diners, startling Rick. His eyes quickly returned to the stand, where he now saw the woman hugging "Katherine," who was obviously the hostess. *Someone's excited,* he thought to himself, giving his watch a quick glance.

"Rick!" the same lady called in his direction as she released the hostess.

Rick met her cheerful gaze and mustered up as much enthusiasm as he could. "Michelle!" he responded, realizing it was his lunch companion who had offered the enthusiastic greeting. *She sure is happy. Is she getting married or something?*

"Rick, this is Katherine," Michelle said as she introduced the hostess. "Her son was just awarded a football scholarship to Ohio State. Katherine, Rick is in real estate, and he'll have to fill me in on the rest of his life before I can tell you anything more." Rick shook Katherine's hand and offered his congratulations.

She blushed and turned to Michelle. "Your usual spot?" Katherine asked.

"Please!" Michelle answered with a smile, and Katherine escorted the pair to one of the private booths in the back corner of the large dining room.

"Josh mentioned that this was a nice place," Rick said as he sat down and scanned the menu. "I see it from the highway all the time, but I'd never been in."

"You've *got* to try the crab cakes. They're fantastic," Michelle said, still all smiles. *Is she really that happy that this hostess's kid got a football scholarship?* Rick briefly studied the woman across the table from him. She was wearing a black wool pantsuit and a black rubber bracelet on her left wrist. She looked more or less his age. He had known plenty of "peppy" girls—especially fifteen years ago in college—but Michelle seemed nothing like them. She was clearly a professional, but animated by an energy that defied his ability to categorize: a lot different from the kind of mortgage person who usually took him to lunch.

"I'm glad you had the time to get together," she continued, breaking into his thoughts. "So how are things going for you?"

Rick felt the muscles in the back of his neck tighten involuntarily, as his polite smile melted away. "Great," he answered mechanically, looking back at the menu. He felt the urge to yawn, but suppressed it. *Maybe I'll go back home after this and take a nap.* As if reading his thoughts, the waitress approached their table with a coffeepot and took their drink orders.

"Hi, Michelle," the waitress said with a smile. "Who's this lucky guy?"

"Jo Ellen!" Michelle scolded jokingly. "This is Rick Masters. He's in real estate. Rick, Jo Ellen is getting her degree in fashion design. Isn't that great?"

"Yeah," said Rick, a little taken aback. *Was Michelle some sort of local celebrity? Why did everyone here seem to know her?* They ordered their drinks, and Jo Ellen departed. The pair was silent for a moment.

"So, you were telling me that business was great," Michelle reminded him softly. Her voice made him think of his older sister when she called to make sure he was eating healthy and exercising.

"Yeah, right," Rick laughed. "I guess it really depends on which answer you want—mine or the company's. I'm not trying to ruin anyone else's day with my problems." Rick wanted nothing more than to return to bed, not that he had been sleeping well recently.

"I don't mind," Michelle offered gently. "We all have problems now and then." *There's that smile again.*

"Well, problems seem to be the norm for me," Rick sighed, scanning her face to see how much he should reveal. Was he really about to spill his guts to a lender? It went against his every instinct, but there was something disarming about Michelle's manner. *What do I have to lose?* "The truth is, things are tough right now. Like everyone else, we were killing it a few years back. Now the market is killing me." Michelle nodded sympathetically and took a sip of her water. "I mean, I used to complain if a listing was on the market for more than three weeks," he continued. "Now I've got properties that have been sitting around for months. I'm taking buyers out to look, and

I'm thinking, *these people aren't serious!* I'm basically a glorified tour guide right now, and..." Rick stopped abruptly. *Okay, that's enough. More than enough, actually.* He looked up to see Michelle's reaction.

A cloud moved in the breeze outside the large front window, and the room seemed to darken. Jo Ellen returned with bread and salad and said, "Oh Michelle, Katherine just gave directions to the gentleman meeting you at 2:00. I just wanted to let you know."

"First time here?" Rick asked sarcastically. Michelle smiled. As he thought about everything he had just revealed, he added weakly, "Sorry, didn't mean to turn this into a confessional."

"Don't worry about it," Michelle assured him. "Look, you know I'm a lender. I've had plenty of agents grin and tell me that this was their best year ever, so I'm glad I don't look that stupid to you!" She laughed. It was a nice laugh, not giddy or boisterous. *What's the word? Genuine.*

"Yeah, I never thought I'd see the day." Rick shook his head. It actually felt good to let it out. "It used to be so easy. A buyer would call. You'd show them around. They'd buy. They needed to sell, so you listed their home. You put a sign in their yard and it would sell. Those days are gone, let me tell you. And don't even get me started on Internet leads. I've gotten so many e-mails from Mickey Mouse, I don't think I ever want to visit Disneyland again! Honestly, Michelle, I think I'm about done."

Geez, am *I done? I always said I'd die before I'd go back to accounting...*

Michelle smiled again. "Well, *I* hope you're not done."

"Why's that?" Rick asked with surprise. *What can I possibly do for her, with my zero leads and my listings languishing on the market?*

"Because markets rise and fall all the time. We all know that. But there are some things money can't buy: reliability, integrity, all that good stuff," she smiled, taking a bite of her salad. "It's not every day I meet an agent who was referred to me by a client who graded that agent a ten out of ten. Josh was very impressed with you."

Rick felt his mood begin to lift. *I knew he liked me, but I didn't realize he ranked me a ten.* He was starting to feel glad he had taken Josh's advice to meet Michelle. He felt himself begin to relax.

"Well, I guess you guys are hurting on the mortgage side too, right?" he asked, expecting that it was Michelle's turn to unload. "A loan officer I know from college just told me last week that he had to give up and go work for the IRS! So what about you?"

"Well, which answer do you want—the company's or mine?" Michelle laughed. Rick laughed too and felt his shoulders relax a little.

"Hey, I thought we were spilling our guts here!" Rick retorted, leaning back in his chair and throwing his hands up in mock offense.

"Yes, yes, of course," Michelle assured him. "The truth is we're actually doing very well with one exception."

"What's the exception?" Rick asked curiously. *Very well? No wonder she's in such a good mood. She has to be the only one in this industry doing "very well."*

"I'm looking for ways to help local agents market our new first-time home buyer programs. Would you mind opening the door at your brokerage for me to do a "Lunch and Learn" seminar at your office? I'll buy the lunch, of course."

"No problem," Rick answered. *She can buy the whole office lunch and that still won't create any leads.* "So what do you teach in your seminar?"

"Well, we offer all kinds of instruction," Michelle explained. The question seemed to light a spark of excitement. "Of course we educate agents on the types of loans we offer, but we also teach effective client follow-up, lead generation techniques and things like that. I usually just ask my contact what the biggest challenge is for agents in the office."

Rick's eyes had opened wide when he heard her mention lead generation, but he was determined to play it cool. "So you guys are really doing well right now?" he asked casually.

"Well, I'm really grateful, because I know it's been tough for a lot of good folks. But actually, we're on pace to double our business from last year, which was up significantly from the year before that," Michelle said modestly.

"That's impressive! What are you doing?" he said, trying not to sound too impressed. He and Michelle had crossed paths over the years, but he had never pegged her as anyone remarkable. Like most agents, he had a love-hate relationship with home lenders. They were an integral part of the business, but he could never shake the feeling that they were all just leeches who wanted to profit off his hard work. Yet he felt Michelle's words piercing through his protective layers of cynicism despite his best efforts to resist. *I think she is actually telling me the truth. Why the heck would she care, though?*

"Well, we're doing lots of things," Michelle explained, taking a sip of her tea. "I'll be happy to go over some stuff in more detail in a minute. But before I forget, Jay Michaels is coming to town this Friday. Why don't you come as my guest? It's normally pretty expensive to attend, but I think I can get you a ticket."

At that moment, Jo Ellen returned with their entrees.

"I'm sorry, but who is Jay Michaels?" Rick had no idea what she was talking about and the smell of his food had caught his attention.

"He's the guy who taught me about the Generosity Generation, which is the whole philosophy of our company," Michelle explained, taking a bite.

"Generosity Generation?" Rick asked apologetically. *Geez, I'm out of it . . . but these crab cakes are great.*

"Basically, it means the more you give, the more you get. Jay shows business people like you and me how to turn our relationships into referrals. There's no catch," she added, perceiving his skepticism. "It's just a really good system. You know how some say it's all about who you know, and some say it's all about who knows you? Well Jay says it's about who you know, how well you know them and who THEY know. Like, Jo Ellen? She's in school so she's not buying right now, but she referred her sister to me. Her sister had a great experience and referred her neighbor who was refinancing. I would have never gotten that business if I hadn't learned how from Jay and my coach."

"Oh," Rick responded. Katherine smiled at both of them as she escorted another couple to the adjacent booth. *I bet that hostess gave her business too.*

As they both ate, Michelle talked freely about her business and her life: she was getting to know some great people, and she seemed to have an endearing story about each of them. She also seemed to be speaking a foreign language using terms Rick had never heard: she mentioned the Generosity Generation again and said something about a Communication Pyramid and the Influential Zone. She spoke about making 1st & 10 calls and communicating her solutions to her community. Rick nodded, but felt himself losing track of what she was saying. Overall, though, he knew she felt confident about where her business was going, even in a down market, and that her life was more balanced and fulfilling than it had ever been.

"I mean, even with market ups and downs, you have to admit this is an incredibly exciting time to be in the business," Michelle said.

"What do you mean?" Rick asked, honestly confused. *Exciting?*

"That's what the Generosity Generation is all about," Michelle explained. "In the old days, the only way to get business was cold-calling, door-knocking, and other ways to 'market to strangers'. Everybody spent time and money trying to attract and close people they'd never met. In the Generosity Generation, we can spend our time, energy, effort, and money on people we actually like and trust. In the end, those are the ones who are most valuable to our business." Rick considered this. Michelle was so animated and energetic as she spoke, but instead of feeling irritated, he felt intrigued. *How can she have so much passion for this stuff?*

"Connecting with people has never been easier," Michelle continued. "The more people I connect with, the more people think of me as a 'mover and shaker.' The more people think of me that way, the more people I connect with. It grows itself and I don't get hung up on or a door slammed in my face. "

"Can you give me an example of something specific which you're doing that's different?" Rick asked.

"Well, I could give you lots of examples. Like just this morning, instead of clipping articles to send to clients like the old days; I used Google Alerts to stay in touch with all my clients and referral partners, and remind them how much I care about them. It doesn't cost me anything and takes no time. The Google Alert comes in, I review it, and then I forward it to the person in my database with a short e-mail from me. I set up a Google Alert for all my referral partners and top referral sources; I call those people Ambassadors and Champions. It's almost like having staff to keep tabs on the people in my community." She added, seeing the confusion on Rick's face, "Oh, it's really easy. I can show you how to do it in twenty seconds.

Before I do that, just to let you know, I have another appointment coming in at 1:00. That's in about 15 minutes."

"Okay. Thanks," Rick answered. Michelle explained Google Alerts in more detail[1], pulling out her phone and demonstrating the process. Rick thought, *I'd like to set up a Google Alert on Don Dasick to see what he's doing.* Jo Ellen quietly cleared their plates and refilled Rick's coffee without being asked. As they continued to chat, Rick was tempted several times to bring up Don and ask if Michelle had heard anything about him, but he resisted.

"Rick, do you mind if I ask you a business question?" Michelle said.

"Sure, Michelle. Shoot."

"If you had a friend or neighbor who was looking to refinance or buy, who would you recommend?" Michelle asked almost casually.

Rick thought about his neighbor living in the condo downstairs; she had asked, but he hadn't referred her anywhere because he didn't get paid for refinances. He sipped his coffee and thought some more.

"I don't know. The last time I talked to someone about refinancing, I didn't send her anywhere. Probably should have, but I don't really have a go-to person. I guess I'd have to say I don't know," he finally answered.

"What would it take for me to be that go-to person?" *Good question.*

"I don't know," Rick answered honestly. "I mean, this meeting didn't do you any harm. If you can be successful in this market, you've got to be doing something right. I guess I'd need to learn more about what you're doing to be successful, and more about what loans you do and don't do."

---

1. For the 7 Essential Google Alerts you should set up, please see www.ReferralLibrary.com.

"Great," Michelle smiled gently. "I want to be your go-to person for loans. I don't need all your business. Just give me a few shots per month. And if I'm hearing you correctly, you're saying that if you get to know me and my business better and like what you see, I'd be your go-to person? Am I correct?"

A few shots per month would be all my business. "Yep. That about sums it up," Rick answered as he drained his last bit of coffee. Jo Ellen slipped by silently for the refill.

"Great, thank you for that answer. I've prepared some information for you to learn more about the solutions I provide," Michelle said, sliding a one-page document across the table. "This is another thing I learned from Jay Michaels and Seven Levels. It's called a Spectrum of Solutions and it shows the full range of services I can provide for you and your clients."

Rick glanced down at the brochure and then feeling bold, blurted out, "Look, neither of us makes money when nobody's buying. Clearly you've found the last people in town who are. You're asking me for help, and I appreciate what you said about my reputation. But if you're doing as well as you seem to be, I'd like to know more about what you're doing. Google Alerts and this Spectrum of Solutions page didn't explode your business."

"Well, let me turn that around," Michelle said softly. "What can I do to help you? What do you need right now?"

"Honestly, I need good, solid leads," Rick confessed. "Like I said, I've tried the magazines, newspapers, home journals, Internet advertising, everything. I know I can deliver what buyers need, but I'm just not finding the people who are buying."

"I hear you," Michelle said. "I really think I can help you with that. But first, just come on Friday and we'll talk about it more after that. Once you hear what Jay has to say, what I say will make a lot more sense." *Is she saying she got all this from some seminar?*

"Well, if he really helped you that much, I'll go," Rick decided.

As the two rose to leave, a sharply dressed man approached their table.

"Hi, Michelle," he said. "I saw you from the foyer and I wanted to let you know I was here for our 1:00." The two hugged and Rick noticed Alan tuck a tendril of Michelle's hair behind her left ear. "Alan, this is Rick Masters. He's a real estate agent. Rick, this is Alan Hubble, he's an attorney at Hubble, Rogers, and Spence. I'll be right back, but you two should exchange cards." The men obeyed and made small talk as Michelle slipped off to the ladies' room.

"Hubble, Rogers and Spence," Rick said. "That's downtown, right?"

"Top floor of the Rogers Bank Building," Alan smiled. *Well, good for you*, Rick thought, resisting the urge to roll his eyes. "So how do you know Michelle?"

"Oh, you know, I'm an agent so I know lots of lenders," Rick said nonchalantly.

"Well, she's quite an up and comer," Alan smiled. "Did she tell you the numbers she did this quarter?"

Rick smiled and nodded, trying to think of a way to end the conversation, when Michelle returned.

"Well, it's been a pleasure, Michelle. Nice to meet you, Alan," Rick offered, starting to think about the rest of his day.

"Rick, absolutely!" Michelle smiled. "We talked all business today, but next time I want to hear more about your goals and what you do for fun. I'll see you Friday!"

Fun? Rick watched Alan and Michelle head to their booth before turning towards the door.

"Goodbye, Mr. Masters," Katherine called to him.

"Goodbye!" Rick smiled and called back, surprised at the enthusiasm in his own voice. He reached for his car keys and realized that for the first time in weeks, he no longer felt tired. Maybe he'd head into the office after all.

JAY MICHAELS SPEAKS

"When the student is ready, the teacher will appear."

CHINESE PROVERB

By the time Friday came, Rick was his tired, listless self again. Still, he couldn't back out of this event. Naturally he could think of a million excuses that sounded plausible; but Michelle had left a voicemail, sent an e-mail, and mailed a card reminding him. Canceling now would be beyond tacky, and Rick still prized his integrity even if he felt like his dignity was bleeding to death.

He was shocked to find the convention center parking lot nearly full when he arrived fifteen minutes early. He entered the building and looked around. *I've never seen this place so crowded. There must be something else going on too.* Yet a glance at the signs seemed to reveal that everyone was there for the same event. Not only that, the crowd seemed eerily friendly. People were hugging, exchanging warm handshakes and even kisses on the cheek. It felt more like a family reunion to Rick: someone else's family reunion. *What am I doing here?*

He found the registration table and received his packet from a cheerful young woman. In it he saw a black rubber bracelet just like the one he had glimpsed on Michelle's wrist at lunch. *I hope I can find her.* Rick didn't mind being alone, but something about the intensely friendly conversations around him made him feel left out. He needed Michelle to help him make sense of all this. He examined the black band and was reading it when he felt a tap on his shoulder.

"There you are!" Michelle said, giving him a quick hug. *That was nice. Does she ever not smile?* "I'm so glad you made it!"

"Me too!" Rick said quickly. Truthfully, he had been glad she wanted him to come, even if he felt a little hesitant about being there. "I appreciate all the reminders."

"Well, I think you're really going to enjoy it. Oh, and thanks so much for e-mailing your broker. I called him and we've got the "Lunch and Learn" scheduled."

"Oh, good, it was no trouble really," Rick said, trying to sound casual. "Anyway, I've never seen this place so full."

"I saved you a seat close to the front with me and a few others. Let's head up there before they get started."

Rick followed her into the main auditorium and down towards the stage. *Wow, we're in the "Reserved" seating. I guess she does know some people.* Rick was very glad he was headed there with her, instead of sitting by himself in this crowd.

When they arrived at their section, Rick shook hands with a few new people. *Oh, there's Alan,* he noticed, looking down the row. *What's a lawyer doing here?* Rick felt a small twinge of disappointment that he chose to ignore.

The crowd began to hoot and holler as the lights dimmed and some music began to play. It was strange to feel so much energy at a business event. *Do they think we're at a rock concert or something?*

An introductory video played, which stirred up everyone even further; and finally, Jay Michaels himself jogged to the center of the stage and waved to the crowd. He was of average height and build, dressed in a black suit and mock turtleneck. Rick realized that he had half expected to see a movie star or celebrity athlete emerge. He found himself rising with everybody else to give a thunderous standing ovation. The intensity was reaching a fever pitch with shouts and cheers. Rick felt chills run up his spine, despite himself. It reminded him of the time his high school football team had made the playoffs for the first time in ten years.

"Thank you!" Jay started. To Rick's surprise, instead of quieting down, the roar got louder. The back and forth continued for what seemed like several minutes as Jay continued to greet the crowd and they welcomed him in return.

"Welcome, members of the Generosity Generation!" Jay began. "I am so excited to share the Seven Levels of Communication with you and show you how to go from relationships to referrals. Even veterans and Ambassadors in the crowd will spot many new items tonight as we continually improve our game!" More cheers. *Jeez, these people really love this guy.*

Jay raised his hands and the crowd quieted almost instantly. It was time to get to work. Rick noticed nobody took their seat. Jay continued, "As many of you know, I always start my day and my presentations with affirmations. They focus our minds for the task ahead. Let's get started!"

Oh, great, Rick thought. He had tried affirmations before, staring in the mirror every morning and telling himself he was stronger and better. It had done nothing. *Here goes nothing,* he thought.

Jay passionately said the affirmations and then the crowd repeated them. A loud clap followed each. Rick mouthed along, and glanced to his side to see what Michelle and her row of fans were doing. They were enthusiastically participating, although he caught Alan looking at his BlackBerry several times. *He can't be here for anything but Michelle.*

The affirmations continued. "I do it now!" Jay shouted.

"I do it now!" The crowd responded. CLAP!

"Excellent!" Jay shouted. "I want each of you to take a look at the black rubber bracelet you received in your packet. This is your procrastination-elimination-solution." *My what? Okay* . . . Rick thought. "Do you remember when your teacher made you write something on the chalkboard over and over when you misbehaved? My teacher made me write phrases like, 'I will not pull Cindy's hair' and 'I will not chew on my pencil in class'. She made me write those things so that it would be instilled in my mind to do the right thing. I want these wrist bands to instill a sense of urgency in you. If your buyers aren't buying and your sellers aren't motivated to sell, perhaps it is YOUR sense of urgency that is lacking, not theirs."

Rick thought about that for a moment. *MY sense of urgency?* For all this noise and hype, Jay had cut right to the chase. Rick felt oddly alert in response.

"To conquer procrastination, this band will remind you to DO IT NOW!" Jay continued. "Tap your band right now and say to yourself, 'Do it now.'"

Everyone tapped his or her band and shouted, "DO IT NOW!" Rick repeated the line along with everyone else. Another thunderous clap followed.

"Again!" Jay implored.

Rick tapped the band on his wrist. "DO IT NOW!" the crowd shouted and then clapped. They did it five more times with each shout and clap getting louder.[2]

"Affirmations—what a great way to start!" Jay continued. "Please have a seat. Thank you." The crowd settled in.

"A wise man once said, 'Begin with the end in mind.' What's interesting about the philosophy of the Seven Levels is that the

---

2. For wristbands and the Do It Now Procrastination Elimination Exercise, please see www.7LSystem.com.

first thing you look at is the end . . . your end. It sounds horrible, but we are all mortals and will someday face our end. We need to make sure our lives AND our businesses are aligned with the legacy we want to leave. To draw a line from point A to point B, we need to know where point B is and what it looks like. Consider these questions: If there were only twelve words written on your tombstone, what would you want them to be? Who would you want at your funeral? What would you want them to say about you?"

Rick shuddered. *Who would come to my funeral if I died today?* The thought was a terrible one. Rick didn't want to pursue it further but he couldn't resist. Did this really have anything to do with his business?

"What you want said about you at your funeral has everything to do with how you do business today," Jay declared, as if in answer to Rick's question. "Your business should be a vehicle for helping you live and leave a legacy. Your business should help you fulfill your purpose. The most important conversation you ever have is the one with yourself. Your affirmations are statements of who you are and who you will be. They shape the kind of business you will run and in turn the type of life you will lead." As Rick pondered this, Jay began telling a story about cold calling, spamming and door-knocking which was getting a lot of chuckles. Rick had never thought of his business as much more than a way to make a living, much less a "legacy." The thought of his funeral continued to bother him.

"Like most of you, my brokers told me the only way I could succeed in this business was to be a spammer, a solicitor or a criminal!" Jay declared to roars of laughter. "I knew I had to find a better way."

Well, if you did, I'd love to hear it, Rick thought sarcastically.

"Then I thought about who I had really sold to in the last six months: my mother's cousin, my college roommate's brother and another friend of a friend," Jay continued.

So?

"And the difference hit me: the people I had sold to trusted me. They used me because we had a relationship. I realized that it was my relationships, not my marketing budget that was going to create my future."

Rick considered his point. Josh had used him because of a mutual friend.

"I stopped chasing leads. I decided not to spend another dime on advertising. I decided to be like a lighthouse that attracts, guides, and directs instead of running all over the place pursuing clients. Guess what happened?"

You burnt out, Rick chuckled to himself.

"I doubled my business . . . every year . . . for four straight years!" The crowd cheered.

Sure, if I had a ton of friends and relatives all over the place, I could make a killing selling to all them too.

Jay went on, "When is a lighthouse most necessary? When there is a storm. We look for a lighthouse when we need guidance and direction, and especially during a storm."

I see where this is going. He's trying to say his system will make you shine in "economic" storms . . .

"Look, the press loves the high winds and rough seas. It's nothing personal, but nobody rushes to buy a magazine or watch a special report on how safe and wonderful everything is. Fear is a powerful motivator and fear sells ads!"

Rick had never really thought of it that way. True, times were tough. But how much of his perception was shaped by the media? He would have to consider that.

"Listen to that quiet voice inside: you know what those news reports are saying doesn't affect you!"

It doesn't?

"Look, you can't control the national or global economy, but you have total control over your personal economy and your attitude. You can lose your car, your job, your home . . . all your stuff. It could happen. But what do you have that no one can take away?"

What do *I have?*

"Your knowledge, your relationships, your family, your love for others, your health, your faith and your happiness. Those are yours. They don't depend on economic conditions. They don't depend on the market. They depend on you. "

Rick thought about that.

"I started to do the math of what a business based on referrals, introductions and connections could look like. I know you were told there would be no math" – the crowd laughed—"but this may be the most important math you've ever seen. Let's say you have 150 people in your database. Raise your hand if you have at least 150 people in your database."

Rick raised his hand and looked around the room. Nearly every person had his hand up. "Now, every business has a turnover rate. For example, the National Association of REALTORS® estimates that the average person moves one out of every five years. So that means one-fifth or twenty percent of your database—thirty people—moves each year.

"If you did thirty transactions last year, you would be in the top ten percent of all real estate agents nationwide," Jay continued. "And when you think about it, if those people sold and then bought, that's sixty transactions a year from a database of only 150 people." The crowd murmured. Rick hadn't thought about his database in months. He had started it in some software program and then started collecting business cards and keeping them in a shoebox. *I doubt I can get sixty transactions out of that box.*

"But where it really gets interesting," Jay went on, "is with the folks that the people in your database know. The average wedding has about 250 people invited, but we'll say that everyone you know is connected to 150 other people. So 150 times 150 is 22,500 and that is your Community. If you're a real estate professional and twenty percent of your Community is moving, then 4500 people in your Community are moving. Folks, that is 9000 transactions! And that's with a database of just 150 people!"

Did I hear that right? Jay repeated the figure and Rick took out a notepad and started jotting down what he was saying.

"Now before we break, let's hear from an Ambassador who is implementing some of the strategies of the Seven Levels. Ladies and gentleman: Janice Weinberger!"

A tiny lady—she had to be less than five feet tall— stood up and appeared on the screens. *She must be sixty!* Rick tried to imagine what this woman could possibly have to say to such a large crowd. He thought about checking his texts.

Janice spoke, "I just want to say that I am living proof that you're never too old of a dog to learn new tricks. I have been a real estate agent for thirty years." Rick's ears perked up. "I absolutely love helping first-time buyers get into homes and start building wealth. After years of blasting neighborhoods with six weeks of postcards and getting maybe one or two calls, most of them angry calls . . ." Rick laughed along with the audience. *I remember those calls.*

". . . I decided to give my coach's methods a try. I focused on one apartment complex where I knew that rents were going up and there were affordable homes nearby. I wrote each of those renters a handwritten note letting them know that when they decided to look for a home, I wanted to be their gal. I let them know I was having a home buyer seminar and invited them to come." The crowd murmured, waiting to hear what happened.

"I'm here to tell you that out of 350 people — yes, I wrote 350 handwritten notes—I had 77 respond—77! And ten of them let me know that they were sorry they couldn't attend but wanted to learn more! Six months later, I am still working with some of those people that called." The audience clapped and a few stood up. Rick wanted to stand up too. *What a great idea!* "The lessons of the Seven Levels work. No matter what your age, you can become a member of The Generosity Generation. Thank you, Jay," Janice finished.

Thunderous applause followed as Jay announced the break.

Rick looked at his notes and took a deep breath as the crowd began to get up and mingle. As he glanced up from his seat, he saw Michelle standing near him. He smiled and stood up. "Wow, this is really something . . ." he offered, not really sure what to say.

"I know," Michelle replied, clearly pleased with his response. "And this is just the tip of the iceberg. I can't wait for you to see the Communication Pyramid and The Upward Spiral of L.I.F.E . . . Before I forget I want to introduce you to a couple of people. You remember Alan of course." Alan looked up from his BlackBerry and offered his hand again.

Rick said, "Sure, from EVT." His voice involuntarily deepened as he spoke.

"Yeah," Alan answered. Then he turned to Michelle abruptly. "Listen, I'd better get going. I just got a message that the firm needs a brief filed by Monday morning. You know I have tickets to the game tomorrow, so . . ."

"Oh that's okay," Michelle said kindly. Rick thought he detected disappointment in her voice. She gave Alan a hug goodbye and introduced Rick to Jeff Schmidt, a chiropractor; and Christy Sutton, a network marketer. After a little conversation, Rick found out that everybody had met with Michelle last Tuesday at EVT Restaurant. *Huh, she's really getting it done.*

Rick remembered what she had said about being perceived as a mover and shaker. He looked down again at his pages of notes and thought about the homework Jay had assigned them. Normally, Rick would have ignored a presenter's "action items," but this time he felt strangely motivated to look at his database.

The lights began to dim again, alerting everyone that the break was about to end. Rick strode back to his seat quickly. *This is actually helpful. Could there be a different way of doing business? I bet Don doesn't know half this stuff...* Rick felt a pang of humiliation in the pit of his stomach as he tried in vain to put that conversation with Don out of his mind. *"Rick, to be honest with you, I don't think you'll be in the business a year from now."* He was relieved to see the crowd settle down and Jay Michaels jog to the stage to loud cheers and applause.

"Okay, guys," Jay resumed, "Now it's time for the Communication Pyramid you've heard so much about. I need everyone here to stand up. Some of you know what's coming but I know you'll indulge me anyway." Rick stood up along with the crowd.

"Great. There is only one rule for this game: you have to be completely honest. Now I want you to imagine that you have no plans for next Friday. You open your morning paper tomorrow and you see a full page ad with a picture of Donald Trump saying, 'I want you to attend my upcoming event in your city.' If you are 100% certain you will attend that event, based on seeing that ad, I want you to sit down now." Rick kept standing. He looked around. Everyone else was still standing too. *Where is he going with this?*

"Really?" Jay laughed. "C'mon, guys, this is the most famous man in real estate and he ran a full page ad to get you to come to his event. Now what if you got a jumbo postcard in the mail with the same picture and the same message? Any affect on those Friday plans? Sit down if that's going to get you there." Rick remained standing. He thought he saw someone sit down out of the corner of his eye, but he couldn't be sure.

"And what if you got an e-mail inviting you to the event?" Jay continued. "Would that make you absolutely certain to go?" Rick saw a guy near the back sit down and a woman sit down near the center aisle. "Sure, you might. After all, he might not make it out this far too often. He might sign your book . . . it could be fun!" The crowd chuckled.

"Now let's say you got a hand-addressed note from a re-turn address you don't recognize," Jay said. "You open the envelope, flip open the card, and there is a handwritten note from Donald Trump. He asks you to attend his event that is coming soon to your city. You lick your thumb and wipe the ink, confirming that it was original. If you knew beyond a reasonable doubt that the note had come from Donald Trump, would you go?" Rick saw that more than half the room was now sitting down.

Jay continued with a smile, "Now you're at work and your receptionist says you have a call. You hear that familiar voice say, 'This is Donald Trump. I only have a minute here, but I wanted to invite you to an event I'm having in your city. Can I count on you to attend?' Now if that happens, and you know you're not part of a prank, how many people in this room would be at that event? Rick sat down along with many others. *A phone call from Donald Trump? Sure, I'm there . . .*

"And for you holdouts," Jay laughed, "What if you came out of your office to find Mr. Trump himself in your waiting area. He shakes your hand, tells you about the event and asks you to come. Will that get you there?" The crowd murmured loudly as every last person sat down.

Jay hesitated to let the point sink in. The crowd was murmuring.

"Okay, that got all of you," Jay said as the crowd quieted down. "So now you see why no one responds to the billboards, or the bus benches or the huge ads. You wouldn't respond to that, and neither will they. Yet you just heard how many people responded to my friend Janice over there, when she took the time to write each of the people in that apartment complex. Because you see, to the people in that apartment complex, Janice is their Donald Trump! She doesn't have a TV show, but she is the gal getting it done in their community! She showed she cared enough to write personally and offer to help. How many of you found out about THIS event by a handwritten note, phone call, or in-person invitation? "

Every hand went up in the room. Rick was floored. It was so true! All those cold calls, all those newspaper and magazine ads: they never worked. They never generated any decent leads. *I've been wasting so much time and money . . .*

"Well, I know we didn't run a single ad. I think you guys are starting to get it!" Jay laughed. Jay continued moving through some slides, further explaining the Seven Levels of Communication and the Communication Pyramid and Rick took notes as fast as his pen would allow him.[3]

"Now before we let you go tonight, you're going to be offered the opportunity to invest in yourself by signing up for coaching. I think almost all of you can see that this is more than anyone can absorb and implement in one night." *You got that right.* "So there are two more people I want you to hear from. Like Janice, they came to a conference just like this. And like Janice, they signed up for coaching. The first is a mortgage professional that was ready to throw in the towel just under a year ago. Everyone, welcome Michelle Phillips."

To Rick's shock, Michelle rose from their row and walked up on stage and stood next to Jay. *Jeez, did she get taller?* Seeing

---

3. See Figures 2-1 through 2-4 at the end of this chapter.

the woman he had just chatted with so casually addressing a crowd of this size felt almost surreal.

"Thanks, Jay!" Michelle said. *She looks so confident!* "I have been coached for about seven months now and it's been an incredible experience."

"Michelle, tell us how things are going and about some of the strategies that you've implemented under your coach's leadership," Jay said.

"Well, Jay, in a market that was down 40% in number of sales and 20% in sales price, we've INCREASED our business by 78% in transactions and our volume by 49%. Most of that came in the last six months of the year. I've increased my income by over $100,000 in the last six months. " Rick joined the crowd in applauding. "One of the most important factors in your homeownership experience is your relationship with your neighbors. Even in today's fast-paced world, we need to take the time to get to know the people around us," Michelle continued. "So now we throw a housewarming party for every one of our buyer-clients as a way to meet those neighbors."

"How does that work?" Jay asked with genuine interest.

"Well, we throw them a party thirty to forty-five days after closing. That timeframe seemed to work best. We cater the food, put out branded signs and take a picture with our clients in front of the house with a sold sign. My coach also suggested that we give out door prizes so that each guest fills out a door prize entry form. That's how we get information for follow-up and ask for referrals. We get three or four referrals on the door prize entry forms at every party."

"Wow, that's a great idea," Jay said, and the crowd applauded in agreement. *That* is *a great idea.* Rick's mind was filling with possibilities. Why hadn't he thought of that before? "What does it generally cost you?" Jay asked.

"Between 200 and 300 dollars for food, but I'm lucky enough to have several partners in my business who help me with the cost for the party. I used to be really shy . . ." *Yeah, right,* Rick thought. "And I was still coming out of that shell when we did our first few parties. My coach suggested I put myself in the role of a server. As soon as I did that at the parties, not only did I feel more comfortable, but I got more referrals!"

"Did you have any challenges with this model at first?" Jay asked.

"Oh, sure," Michelle laughed. "We used to wait until closing to ask the clients if they wanted to do a housewarming party. That didn't go over so well when they were stressed out about moving. So after some trial and error we got smarter and began explaining the housewarming party at the initial consultation instead of waiting until closing. We just made it a part of the process. You get pre-approved, make an offer, get a contract, sign papers at closing, then host a housewarming party."

"And your coach has helped you refine your model?" Jay inquired.

"Oh yes," Michelle confirmed. "Coach is never satisfied. Our system was pretty good four months ago. Then my coach showed me how to use some of the concepts from the Communication Pyramid to take the parties to the next level. First, he suggested that I call all invitees to confirm that they would be attending. We were sending nice invitations out and I felt that was enough. I figured it was up to the buyer-client to get them there. But my coach kept emphasizing that we wanted to immerse ourselves in our buyer-clients' circle of friends. To maximize my time, I needed to get as many as possible to that party. So I began calling to confirm and attendance soared. Instead of getting 50% or less, we are now getting more than 75%. And with more people, the energy is also higher. The clients seem to enjoy themselves more. These parties are a lot of fun!⁴"

"So it sounds like this is a big reason you've seen such growth in your business while others are seeing declines," Jay offered.

"Absolutely. Coaching helped me understand how to implement what I was learning about the Seven Levels. The ideas are simple and inexpensive but very powerful. I definitely wouldn't be where I am without these principles and my coach's help in putting them into practice."

"Thanks, Michelle," Jay smiled and Rick joined the crowd in applauding as she made her way down the side stairs and back to her seat. Rick caught a glimpse of her smile. She looked almost radiant. *Wow! Go Michelle!*

"Michelle's success is a great reminder of how cultivating a few deep relationships is better than accruing thousands of shallow relationships. Someone else who understands this concept is one of our youngest coaching clients. At 22 years old, Jeremy has a blossoming landscaping business and he doesn't spend a penny on advertising. He doesn't even have a yellow pages ad. He's as busy as you can get and has hired ten new people in the last six months. Everyone, welcome Jeremy Stahl."

Rick watched a young man walk across the stage and take the microphone that Michelle had just held. He was shorter than average and wore jeans and a bright blue button-down shirt with his company logo on the chest pocket. *He's just a kid!* Rick thought.

"Thank you, Jay. Great to be here. My dad thought I was crazy to spend so much money on coaching," Jeremy's voice affectionately imitated his father's country accent—"'why in tarnation are you going to pay someone to tell you what to

---

4. To get a copy of the New & Improved Housewarming Party System, go to www. ReferralLibrary.com.

do?'" The crowd laughed in response. "But in my gut, I knew I needed help to take my business to the next level. My dad is the best man I know and he taught me everything I know about landscaping, but he never took the business beyond putting food on our table and keeping a roof over our heads. I knew we could do better than that."

"So how did it happen for you, Jeremy?" Jay asked.

"I had met an older gentleman at a networking function who was a golf course grounds' consultant. I knew this guy was the real deal, so I asked my coach on how to maximize the contact. We put together a plan. I had already written "Birdie"— that's what they call him—a handwritten note immediately after meeting him. I had also put a P.S. in there for him to call me. He did call, and we chatted a little bit and set up a follow up time for coffee. I put him into one of my Tuesday afternoon networking slots. We met and it went great. Then my coach and I worked it out to get him onto Lionbrooke." Rick raised his eyebrows. Lionbrooke was the most exclusive golf course in the region and was known worldwide.

"Coach and I then took our plans to the next level. I found out his grandson, Wyatt, is a fantastic golfer at the local high school, so I set up a tee time for the three of us and had a limo pick up Birdie and his grandson. I sat in the back and greeted them. They loved it. Heck, I loved it." The crowd buzzed with approval.

"I don't remember how we shot. It didn't matter. It was a fantastic day."

Jay prodded him on, "The story doesn't end there. Keep going, Jeremy."

"Well, it was going the extra mile, but in reality, the whole day including tips cost me less than $2000. I would never have even thought about all this without my coach's pushing. And it only gets better. I followed up with a handwritten note to both of them, thanking them for their time. Two weeks later, I got a call. Birdie had ten golf courses that needed landscape architecture work done, this fall. That could be nearly one million dollars in business! But there's more. Birdie had struck up a conversation with the pro at Lionbrooke and now he was going to do some consulting with that course too. Lastly, Wyatt qualified for the high school state championship and guess where that tournament was played this year? Yes, Lionbrooke. And you guessed it, Wyatt won. Folks, I know this is hard to believe. Believe me this stuff is too crazy to make up."

Jay looked like a proud papa as he applauded. "Let's give a big hand to Jeremy. What an outstanding story about the power of going deep with relationships! Give yourself an action item to put together a *Go Deep Day* for one of your Ambassadors within the next 60 days. Believe me, it will be worth every penny.

"Now before I let you go, I want to share something with those of you who might be having a rough year." Rick looked up expectantly. "I want you to know that there is only one difference between Jeremy, who just had his best year ever, and you. There's only one difference between Janice, or Michelle and you. And that is that they are just failing at a higher level." Many in the audience laughed. *What is he talking about?* Rick wondered. *None of them look like they're failing at all.*

"All of us know what a downward spiral in life is. Things go from bad to worse until they're spinning out of control. Well I want to close tonight by reminding you of the Upward Spiral of L.I.F.E. LIFE stands for Learn, Implement, Fail, Evaluate." Rick jotted this down as quickly as he could, as Jay showed no sign of slowing down.

"Imagine a spiral staircase," Jay continued. "The only way to climb each step is to go through this process: Learn, Implement, Fail, Evaluate. Every honest person knows that failure is a part of life. But if you learned anything tonight and you implement it, then when you fail next, you will fail at a higher level. When you evaluate that failure, you will find yourself on the next step in that upward spiral. And those who are top producers not only fail, but they fail faster. Learn, Implement, Fail, Evaluate. The Upward Spiral of L.I.F.E. will take you higher than you've ever dreamed."

As Jay wrapped up the conference with some closing remarks, Rick was deep in thought. This evening had offered him the most useful advice and ideas that he could remember getting, but he knew there was no way he could turn his business around by himself. He *did* need accountability, or he would continue doing what he'd been doing for the last eighteen months.

I can't afford coaching. I can't afford coaching. The thought repeated itself in his brain like a scratched CD. There were no two ways about it: bills were piling up and no matter how good these ideas were, he didn't have any leads right now.

Rick smiled weakly at Michelle who was busy talking to a long line of people who had gathered in response to her impressive testimonial. She waved back apologetically and continued to attend to her fans. Yet Rick thought he caught a glimpse of genuine concern on her face.

It was useless to debate it anymore. Rick knew what he needed to do. As he picked up his briefcase, he became strangely aware of how fast his heart was beating and how sweaty his palms had become. With a grim resolve, he headed over to a large table already mobbed by attendees. Rick reached for his wallet and pulled out the credit card he had vowed to use only for emergencies.

THE SEVEN LEVELS OF COMMUNICATION

COMMUNICATION PYRAMID

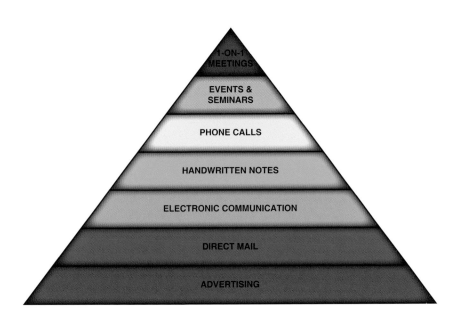

FIGURE 2-1: THE COMMUNICATION PYRAMID DEPICTS THE SEVEN LEVELS OF COMMUNICATION FROM THE BOTTOM LEVEL ADVERTISING TO THE TOP LEVEL ONE-ON-ONE MEETINGS. SEE 7 STEPS TO A SUCCESSFUL SUCCESS STORY AT www.REFERRALLIBRARY.COM

THE SEVEN LEVELS OF COMMUNICATION

COMMUNICATION PYRAMID

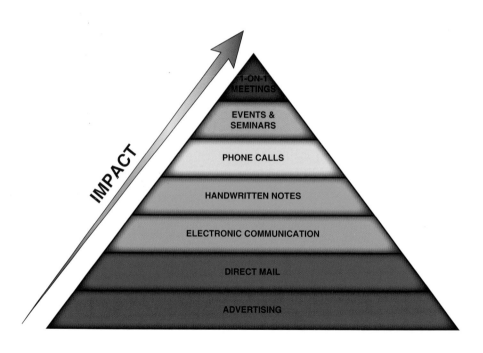

FIGURE 2-2: AS THE DONALD TRUMP EXAMPLE SHOWS, AS YOU GO UP THE PYRAMID, YOU HAVE MORE IMPACT ON THE OTHER PERSON AND THE RELATIONSHIP GROWS STRONGER (SEE IMPACT ARROW).

THE SEVEN LEVELS OF COMMUNICATION

COMMUNICATION PYRAMID

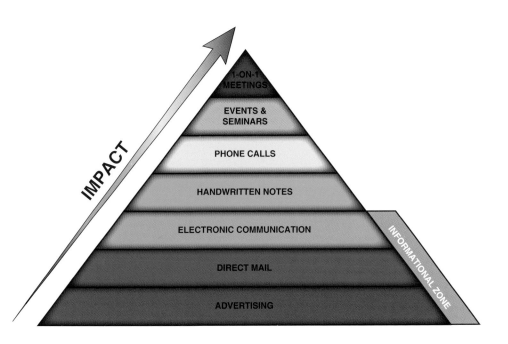

FIGURE 2-3: THE LOWER THREE LEVELS ARE THE INFORMATIONAL ZONE.
THESE TYPES OF COMMUNICATION ARE BEST USED FOR INFORMING,
CONFIRMING, OR UPDATING. SEE SUCCESS STORIES.

THE SEVEN LEVELS OF COMMUNICATION

COMMUNICATION PYRAMID

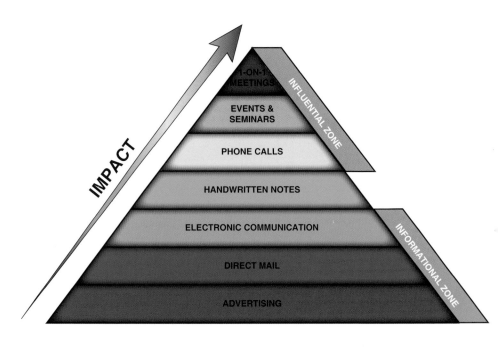

FIGURE 2-4: The upper three levels are the Influential Zone. If you are looking to influence, convince, or sell, do it with Phone Calls, Events & Seminars, or One-on-One Meetings.

COMMUNICATING WITH YOURSELF

3

"THANKS FOR MEETING ME, Michelle," Rick said as he brought two large coffees to their corner table.

"No problem," she assured him, taking her cup. For a moment Rick thought of her on stage at the conference again, the crowd hanging on her every word. Yet here she was having coffee with him. Pretty cool, actually.

"I know you're busy but I didn't really know who else to call," he offered apologetically. It was true. Brian was probably his best friend, and it had been ages since they'd hung out. The rest of his Friday night drinking buddies had gone the way of the dinosaur when he stopped buying their drinks. "Well, I'll get right down to it. I think I might have made a mistake by signing up for coaching..."

"What makes you say that?" Michelle asked, unfazed. *Jeez, and I was worried about offending her.*

"Well, first of all, there's the money..." Rick began.

"Oh, I totally understand," Michelle assured him. "I know it's not cheap."

"But listen, I understand the money-back guarantee, and I believe the guy when he says he'll give my money back if I don't think these sessions improve my business. I don't think Jay's hurting . . ." They both laughed. "But there's something else. It's hard to explain. But I'm not sure I'm the kind of guy that coaching will work for."

"What do you mean?" Michelle asked gently.

"Well, it's just that I'm a really private person, you know? I'm not all into the touchy-feely stuff the way you guys are."

"Us guys?" Michelle smiled, sipping her coffee.

"You know, the 'Jay Michaels' Generosity Generation.' I mean, I think it's great and everything, but all the high fives and hugs just aren't really my style. I'm the kind of guy that just wants to get things done, you know. Not that you guys aren't getting it done . . ."

"Well, that's the thing," Michelle said softly. "You've honed in on a really important distinction. We *are* different, and that's what makes our system work. But I promise you, it can work for anyone, even a private person." *Did she just wink at me?*

"How can you be sure?" Rick asked doubtfully. It was too embarrassing to tell her that he had approached Don just weeks before for mentorship and he had responded with a dark forecast for Rick's business. If Don who had been around forever thought he was doomed, how would this coach be any different?

"Because look at *me*!" Michelle laughed, as if the answer was obvious. "You heard me at the conference. I used to be deathly shy!"

"Yeah, I have to confess, I have a hard time believing that," Rick chuckled, draining his cup.

"Well, believe it, Mister. I didn't even attend the first house-warming party I set up because I was too nervous! I'm telling you, if coaching can work for me, it can work for you. Especially with the coach you've been assigned to. I made sure you got him." Was there something more in that smile? *No, she's with Alan. I'm sure she is.*

"You did?" Rick asked. *Am I blushing? What is wrong with me?*

"Sure," she smiled. "He's the same guy that worked with me. He's like a dad, or a grandfather. You'll learn to love him, I promise!"

"*Learn* to love him?" Rick raised his eyebrows.

"I'm not going to lie to you: he's tough," Michelle laughed. "But he's great. I'm telling you, he taught me everything I know— well, he and Jay . . ."

"Okay," Rick chuckled, feeling his mood lift a bit. "I'll take your word for it."

"Just think of it this way: what have you got to lose?" Michelle asked. Rick had to admit she was right. If it didn't work, he could always get his money back.

WHAT DO I SAY TO MYSELF?

"Well, Mr. Rick Masters, how are you?" Rick was surprised at the gruff, serious voice that greeted him on the other end of the line. It reminded him of his shop teacher in junior high school.

"Doing fine," Rick said in his best good ol' boy voice.

"Well, I'm not one for small talk, so what say we figure out if this is going to work for you, okay?"

"Okay," Rick was a little taken aback. *This is the guy who taught Michelle everything she knows?*

"Good. I'm going to ask you some questions and you just fire back. Don't try to over-think. Got it?"

"Sure." Rick was not sure what to expect.

"On a scale of 1 to 10, if a 10 gets referrals all the time, where are you?"

Rick thought about it for a moment, "Probably a 5." *Or maybe a 1 or 2.*

"Great. What would it take for you to be a 10?"

"I don't know. These sessions I guess."

"Fair enough. Are you friendly?" Coach continued.

"Sure." Rick wanted to return the question, but kept quiet.

"Are you trustworthy?"

"Yes," Rick replied.

"Okay, last question. Are you willing to put all advertising on the back-burner and focus on building a relationship-based business?" *All advertising? While I still have no leads?* Rick started to feel like he had something to lose after all.

"What about home magazines?" Rick asked, trying to sound casual.

"Cockamamie!" *What did he just say?* Rick thought. "No magazines. No newspapers. No Yellow Pages. No billboards. No advertising!" Coach's voice was firm, but slightly impatient.

"For how long?" *What good is this coaching if I become homeless in the process?*

"Just as long as we're doing this training. There are seven sessions—you know that—and you go at your own pace. So however long it takes you, that's how long you're not advertising. "

Rick had a feeling that "no" was not really an option. "Okay, I guess so."

"Cockamamie!" *Is this guy real? He sounds like a cartoon character . . .* "I mean, are they busting down your door because of the home magazine ads?"

"Well, no . . ."

"Okay, then it won't be a problem. Now you're either in or you're out with this, so what's it going to be?"

"I'm in," Rick said firmly. *What am I doing? Everyone who thought I was finished is going to know it for sure now. Don's going to be like . . .*

"Okay," Coach said, interrupting Rick's thoughts. "Now, Jay wants me to tell you that this call is a sacred space. I'm not one for all the psychobabble," *Me neither!* "But just know that you can say whatever you want when we're on these calls. You're not going to shock me and I'm not going to tell anyone. I've heard it all. I'm not here to tell you that you're a good or bad person, I'm here to help you through the Seven Levels."

"Gotcha."

"Okay, one last thing," Coach said, almost chuckling. "Lots of you kids who sign up for coaching are what I like to call 'education junkies.' You listen to CDs, read every online article you can find on the industry, and have a pile of magazines on your coffee table," *Okay . . .* Rick wasn't sure where this was going.

"Well, while we're working on this, we're going to cut all that off. Just for right now. Save it all and dive right in when we're done, but for now no outside books, no CDs, no magazines, no RSS feeds, no webinars, none of that. Believe me, you're going to have plenty of things to read, watch, and listen to during these sessions. Just make sure you're taking the medicine the doctor orders and not mixing it with anything else. It's about focus, got it?"

"Got it." *Am I joining a cult? Am I allowed to watch the local news to see if it's going to rain?*

THE WHY

"Okay, so let's get going." Coach continued, "Rick, what got you into real estate?"

Rick answered quickly, "Opportunity."

"Opportunity for what?"

Rick thought for a second. "Honestly, for money and independence. I hated my old job. My dad had always told me to become an accountant. Good, safe, white collar job. And I did it. I studied through college, passed the CPA exam and figured out at 26 that I hated going to work every day."

"What did you hate about it?"

"I hated being in an office all day and I hated being told what to do all the time, I guess. My sister knew I was miserable and she told me to try getting my broker's license. She thought it would fit my personality better. I followed her advice and I've never really looked back. And I showed my dad I could make money doing something else."

"But not so much right now?" *Ouch.*

"Yeah, you got me there. I mean, the market's killing me right now. I guess maybe Dad was right . . ." Rick laughed bitterly.

"I don't think so. I think you *are* cut out for this. I just think you'll benefit from a new approach."

"Thanks." Hearing Coach say that felt surprisingly good.

"Well, I assume you've been to a lot of sales seminars in your life," Coach said with a sigh.

"Sure."

"So you already know that to be a good salesman, your 'why' has to be strong enough. When your why is strong enough, the how takes care of itself. For a lot of the guys I talk to, they're out there for their wives and kids. You don't have any of that, do you?"

"Well, no . . ." Rick stammered. *That's getting a little personal.* For a brief moment, Rick wondered why he had never gotten married. Who would it have been? Tracy, Karen, Shawna . . . his last few girlfriends had been great looking and Karen had actually been a lot of fun, but he couldn't picture any of them raising his kids. Since the money had dried up, it had been pretty lonely though. Then a thought occurred to him, "Well, what about you, Coach?" he asked.

"That's really none of your business," Coach said flatly. "But since you asked, yes, forty years last May and her smile and the trust of my two sons and baby girl were my 'why' every day I was out there. I married her the day before I left for Basic Training. I wanted to give them a life that didn't depend on the weather or farm subsidies like my father's did. Did my time here and abroad, got my education and went into sales. We didn't have performance awards and little achievement plaques back then, Rick; just simple commissions. But I knew that woman and those kids were counting on me and I was never going to let them down." Rick was silent. The conviction in Coach's voice was almost overpowering. *Do I care about anything that deeply?*

"So you could win every award there is in real estate and be on the cover of *Forbes* and Dad would still think you failed because you left accounting, right?" Coach inquired.

"Yeah, you're probably right," Rick agreed.

"But that sister of yours; you'd like to make her proud, huh?"

"Yeah, I would . . ." Rick fought the lump rising in his throat. "No offense, but what does this have to do with getting referrals?" he asked sharply.

"Watch it there," Coach warned. "Remember, you're the one who needs this, not me. Mr. Michaels didn't pull me out of retirement to talk to people who don't want to be bothered. I'd just as soon be fishing if you're not going to follow all the way through with this . . ."

"Fair enough," Rick said quickly. "I didn't mean to be disrespectful. I just didn't understand how it connected."

"It's all about the why, Rick. If part of your why is being independent, you'll soon learn that none of us can achieve success on our own. But let's move on. Why don't you tell me what you got out of the conference with Jay? That's why we're talking, right?"

"Yeah, I guess so," Rick said. He thought about what had impressed him so much at the conference, which now seemed very long ago. "Well, I took a lot of notes and the information was much more practical than what I've gotten at a lot of other seminars. The Communication Pyramid, and the number of transactions you should have based on your database: I had never heard that before. But I guess what put it over the top for me was the testimonials. I mean, I knew Michelle already and some of her story, but hearing from that lady and that young guy . . . and I think they're legit because what they did really made sense. Those were great ideas."

"So Michelle, Janice and Jeremy got quantifiable success from their coaching time. Tell me, at the end of these seven sessions, what will quantifiable success look like for you?" Coach asked.

Rick thought. "I'm not totally sure. More referrals, I guess . . ."

"How many referrals are you getting per week now?" Coach asked.

"Per week?" Rick asked, clearing his throat. "Maybe one per month."

"So let's say twelve per year. Let's set a Referral Goal," Coach said. "How many referrals do you want to earn in the next twelve months?"

"Twenty-five?" Rick said hesitantly. *Where was I going to get 25 referrals?*

"Cockamamie, Rick! You need to speak with conviction. Make me believe you believe what you're saying!" Coach commanded through the earpiece. Rick immediately sat up straight.

"Okay, I will try to get 25 referrals in the next twelve months," Rick said in a deeper voice.

"Try?" Coach asked.

"I WILL get 25 referrals in the next twelve months," Rick said with more authority.

"Okay, set it at fifty," Coach prodded. "You will receive fifty referrals in the next 12 months. You WILL. If you don't, we'll give you 100% of your money back. Deal?"

Rick said, "Deal." *That's the deal of the century for me!*

Coach continued by saying, "To get fifty referrals, you will need to consciously give out 100 referrals. You refer inspectors to your buyers, you refer your neighbors to lenders for re-fis, you connect people in your Community with one another, and you refer members of your Community to other agents in other parts of the country. You're now going to look for opportunities to connect people. Right?"

"Right," Rick answered.

He and coach continued to talk for several more minutes, discussing Rick's specific goals and what he hoped to get out of the sessions. He told Rick to create several affirmations for himself which would go on post-it notes on his mirror and something he called a Blessings Book[5] where he would write his affirmations and the five things he was grateful for each morning. Rick rolled his eyes, imagining a pink notebook covered with flowers and unicorns. Then they started talking numbers: Coach asked Rick for a sales goal for the next twelve months and then challenged him to triple it. Rick was stunned to silence.

"I want that number on your mirror, on your computer and in your office," Coach ordered. Then he started talking about physical fitness. *Next he'll tell me I need to be married in six months . . .* Still, Rick knew that he needed to start taking better care of himself.

"Look, if an old guy like me can get up and run five miles a day, then the least you can do is get back to the gym!"

"Fair enough!" Rick laughed.

---

5. For a Blessings Book example, please see www.ReferralLibrary.com.

Coach continued talking, explaining how to break up the rest of Rick's goals into manageable daily tasks. "We need to add one more post-it note to your mirror and one more thing in your Blessings Book," Coach finished. "It's powerful and it's called the Rainmaker's Affirmation: 'Each and every day, someone, somewhere in my city, needs my services. My job TODAY is to find that person.' Internalize this and you'll think like a top producer."

Rick wrote the Rainmaker's Affirmation in his notes capitalizing the word "TODAY". He still wasn't sure about all these affirmations, but he knew from the sound of Coach's voice that they were non-negotiable.

Coach told him to write the twelve-word epitaph he wanted to see on his tombstone and do a vision exercise called The Four Eulogies – what he would want four special people, including a client, to say about him at his funeral. Rick's mind drifted back to Jay's remarks at the conference.

"Look, if my commander wanted me to chart a course through the jungle or the desert from point A to point B, he had to tell me where point B was. Your funeral, like it or not, is point B," Coach pointed out.

"Yeah," Rick said quietly. He still didn't like thinking about his funeral. Coach continued with another item Rick had never considered—The Perfect Voicemail Greeting showed Rick how to take control of his phone calls and freed him up several hours of the day.

"And another thing," Coach added, clearing his throat. "You got your wristband at the conference. You're going to repeat 'Do It Now' to yourself 49 times, 3 times daily[6]."

"What?" Rick asked in disbelief.

---

6. For the Perfect Voicemail Greeting and the DoItNow Exercise Sheet, please see www. ReferralLibrary.com.

"It's about urgency, Rick," Coach explained. "It's hard to make yourself do things. I'm your coach, but I'm not there yelling at you 24/7. This exercise will build your sense of urgency just like curling free weights will build your biceps." *When am I going to find the time to get all this done? Of course without advertising, I won't really be busy showing houses . . .* Rick's heart sank briefly. *What am I going to do if this doesn't work?*

He glanced at his watch and realized that their time was almost up.

"Is that enough homework for you?" Coach chuckled.

"Yeah, definitely." Rick felt a little overwhelmed, but tried hard not to show it.

POWERFUL POWER NOTES

"Okay, now we've got just a few minutes left, so let's talk about those Handwritten Notes. Janice's story impressed you, so I know you'll be willing to try."

"Absolutely," Rick answered. "But I mean is there really all that much to it? I learned how to write a friendly letter in third grade . . ." As soon as he heard the words come out of his mouth, he knew it was a mistake.

"Cockamamie!" Coach blurted out. "If it were that simple all your drinking buddies would be doing it! Listen, there is a wrong way to do this, I promise you. I'm going to save you a whole lot of time and tell you how to do it right. You can either be thankful for that or we can end the call now."

"No, no," Rick apologized. "I just didn't get it, that's all." *Geez.*

"Okay, listen, this is important. Here are the 7 Steps to a POWER Note:"

Rick listened carefully and wrote:

7 Steps to a POWER Note:

1. Use unbranded cards with a symbol or monogram that represents you. It's a personal note.

2. Use blue ink. It looks original and positive.

3. Words - use you, but avoid I, me, my.

4. Be specific in your praise. Identify and acknowledge a characteristic, a talent, a unique quality.

5. Leverage the Power of Positive Projection. Identify a personal characteristic you want to improve and express respect for others who possess that quality (happiness, wealth, balance, etc.)

6. Write rightly - slope text slightly upward from left to right. Read Your Handwriting Can Change Your Life by Vimala Rodgers.[7]

7. The Power of the P.S. Use a P.S. as a call-to-action: ask the recipient to take action such as e-mailing or calling.

"Whom do I write these POWER Notes to?" Rick asked.

"Everybody you know," Coach answered. "Pick up a business card, look in your e-mail, look in your database—find a person, identify a positive characteristic to acknowledge, and write the note. Write as many as you can this week—at least 50. Remember to write a compelling P.S., and your phone will ring."

"What do I say when they call?" Rick asked.

"You'll know," Coach answered without explaining. "We're short on time, but there's one more VERY important topic I want to cover before our time ends today. Do I have your attention? I want to warn you about something."

---

7. Vimala Rodgers, *Your Handwriting Can Change Your Life* (New York: FIRESIDE, 2000). To see a complete list of resources, see www.ReferralLibrary.com.

"Yes," Rick answered affirmatively. *Warn me?*

Coach continued, "I want to warn you about something that will happen as you experience the Seven Levels. It's called Success Suicide."

"Success Suicide?" Rick asked. *I knew it. I am going to have to drink the Kool-Aid!*

SUCCESS SUICIDE

"It's the breakdown before the breakthrough. This has happened to all my clients just as they are on the brink of achieving their goals," Coach explained somberly. "It is real, and it is serious. As you become more successful, something inside you will start to resist that change. You will get sick or injured or something else will happen that will try to sabotage you."

"So what do I do?" Rick was skeptical, but figured it couldn't hurt to ask.

"You persevere. Success Suicide can rear its ugly head in many ways. Many times it is in the decisions you make. On other occasions, it is a physical form of self-sabotage like illness or accidents. You must persevere. This is the all-important breakdown before the breakthrough." Coach said seriously.

"So is this coaching going to work for you, Rick?" Coach asked matter-of-factly.

"Well, I guess that's kind of up to me, isn't it?" Rick offered.

"Very good," Coach said with a hint of approval in his voice. "Do you have everything you need to complete the action items?"

"Yeah, I think so," Rick answered. He felt tired. It had been a lot to absorb and he had a lot of homework to do. He had tons of POWER Notes to write. They said goodbye, and Rick looked at the clock on his wall. It was too late to go into the office anyway. Besides, his alerts had just let him know that Don had sold the home of the former governor to a pro-football player. The last thing he needed was to go in and hear Don regaling everyone with the conquest. Might as well order some carry-out and start on his homework.

I wonder what Michelle's doing tonight . . . Rick stopped the thought as he walked down his street to the corner deli to pick up his dinner. What was going on? *Michelle was not his type at all.* Rick had spent his adult life chasing and catching leggy blondes, with an occasional brunette or a redhead thrown in for good measure. Michelle was, by any objective standard, physically average. Her hair was nice, she had a trim figure but there was nothing about her appearance that would have made him notice her on the street. *Why do I keep thinking about her?*

Rick returned to his condo with his sandwich and mountain of fries and spread everything out on the dining room table. Between bites, he grabbed his pad of notes from the call and examined his action items. What should he start with? Coach had warned him that he had to cancel all his ads within the next three days. The thought made Rick sick to his stomach.

There had to be something else he could work on. Writing his affirmations? Counting his blessings? Creating the epitaph for his tombstone? *That still seems so morbid, even if we are supposed to begin with the end in mind.*

As much as he didn't want to deal with it, writing a POWER Note to Jay and to Coach seemed like the best way to go. He polished off half his sandwich and went into his office to start. He cleared a path through his files and books and picked up the morning paper. As he folded it to throw away, he caught a glimpse of Don's face smirking at him from the real estate section. Suddenly, a thought hit him: *is this an ad for a house or for spray tan?*

Rick laughed out loud. It seemed so bizarre all of a sudden. Why would you make your picture bigger than the house you were trying to sell? He chucked the paper in the trash and found the note cards he had printed a while back.

YOU CAN'T EVEN SPELL COMMUNICATE WITHOUT TIME

"This time, like all times, is a very good one, if we but know what to do with it."

RALPH WALDO EMERSON

R ICK RACED BACK to his condo, morning coffee in hand, and smiled at his neighbor as he unlocked his door. He never had learned how to brew it well. Until a couple of weeks ago, his early morning trip to the coffee shop housed in the bottom of his building had been his most reliable pleasant human interaction. But all that was changing.

As he reached his door, he felt his phone vibrate. It was still a little unnatural for him not to answer. For the first time in months, Rick was busy. He gulped his coffee as he looked at his phone and grabbed his legal pad to make a list of people to call back. He was grateful for Coach's instruction to change his voicemail message. Instead of "I'll get back to you as soon as possible," which Coach had explained was a lie; it now gave the caller specific times when he would return calls. He soon found that Coach was right: he had more freedom by controlling when he made his calls instead of answering his phone every time it rang.

Rick looked at his notepad in horror. He realized there were three, no four, messages from yesterday that he had failed to return. *Ugh! I changed my voicemail message and I'm still lying!*

Not that Rick was upset. Far from it. He was writing POWER Notes to everyone he knew as Coach instructed and people were calling. He had shown three properties yesterday, two the day before and eight last week. It had not even been that long since his coaching call.

Even the affirmations, which still made Rick roll his eyes when he thought about them, were starting to work their magic and he found himself smiling more despite himself. He had a bounce in his step that had been missing for a while. After reading *QBQ: The Question Behind the Question*, watching *The Secret* several times and listening to Napoleon Hill's *Think & Grow Rich*[8]; he knew his attitude had changed. He had a renewed sense of purpose.

Writing his blessings down every morning had made an even bigger difference; Rick had rarely taken the time to consider how much better his life was—even in the toughest of times—than that of so many others. He had a home, he had transportation, enough to eat, and although his family wasn't perfect, they loved him and had provided everything he needed in life. Writing his eulogies had made him appreciate those relationships.

His sister had noticed the difference immediately.

"What's gotten into you, Rick?" his sister asked on their regular Sunday evening call. "You sound, you sound . . ."

"Less miserable?" Rick had interjected with a laugh.

"Yeah! That's it! Who is she?"

Rick wanted to talk to Susan about Michelle, but what was there to say? "No, it's nothing like that. It's just that business is finally picking up. I think this coaching thing was actually a good idea."

---

8. For a complete Referral Resource Library, please see www.ReferralLibrary.com.

"I had a good feeling about it . . ." she had agreed.

"Well that made one of us. But it's definitely what I need right now. The guy knows what he's talking about, despite the fact that he totally sounds like a more sophisticated version of Mr. Winston from shop class, and he e-mails me like twice a day to make sure I'm doing my stuff."

"Mr. Winston? Really?" she laughed "Still that is what you need, Rick. You wouldn't have ever turned in your homework if Mom and I hadn't stayed on your case."

Rick turned back to his legal pad and sighed. Some things never change! His dining room table, which had become his desk since his actual desk in his office was hidden by clutter; was covered with post-its, stacks of e-mail printouts, and the four legal pads he had used up trying to do his homework. Rick shook his head. It was too overwhelming to even think about.

At any rate, the first order of business was to return these calls. He accessed his voicemail and picked up a pen to jot down the information. To his surprise, his hand felt sore. *Ha! Next thing you know, these POWER Notes are going to give me carpal tunnel!* He listened to each message, jotting down the relevant information.

Rick's mind drifted to his upcoming coaching call. He knew Coach was going to ask him who his accountability partner would be, but he was still coming up empty. Brian was way too busy with his third kid on the way, plus they had moved out of the state. None of his other "friends," even if Rick started buying the rounds again, was the right kind of person. He had thought several times about asking Michelle. They were supposed to meet again today at 1:00 to discuss housewarming parties, since Rick had a client closing before the end of the month.

Oh no! Rick looked again at his legal pad: he had just received a message from a new client confirming an appointment today to sign the paperwork for listing her home. *I'm supposed to meet Michelle at 1:00 and the client at the same time!* Rick felt sick. *Double booked!* He hadn't been busy enough to double book before today! *I've got no choice,* he thought sadly. He sighed heavily and picked up his phone.

TIME'S UP

"Hey, Coach," Rick said as their second conference call began.

"Hi, Rick. I'm not too happy with you right now. You wanna guess why?" *Oh, boy.* Rick's stomach sank a bit. *This has not been a good day.*

"Well, I can think of a lot of reasons," he said as lightheart-edly as he could. "But I guess you'd better tell me."

"I got your note and so did Jay. I'm glad you did the assignment. But I told you specifically to use unbranded cards." *Ugh! I can't believe I forgot.* Rick had ordered the cards ages ago and hadn't thought twice about pulling them out. *Is it really that big of a deal?*

"Look. Does your mom send you a birthday card that says 'Mom Industries' on it? What would you think if she did?"

"I get it," Rick apologized.

"Okay. Remember, this is not about looking big. It's about being personal and real. Now let's get down to it. I can tell by the way you're responding to my e-mails that you are flying by the seat of your pants. Am I right?"

"Yeah," Rick admitted.

"Okay, that's going to have to stop. I always say that wherever you are, you need to be there 100%. If you're ripping and running, you're never going to be able to give your clients the attention they deserve and they won't refer you.

"Today is about time. Your first action item is a Vision Exercise. Like The Four Eulogies, this exercise makes you look at the big picture. You're going to imagine your Perfect Workday and write it out from the moment you wake up until the moment you go to bed. Break it down hour-by-hour and describe exactly what you're doing on your perfect workday. Got it?"

"Got it," Rick answered. *No problem.* He had ended up enjoying The Four Eulogies exercise more than he thought he would.

THE INFLUENTIAL ZONE & TIME BLOCKING

"Rick, do you remember which three levels of the Communication Pyramid comprise the Influential Zone?" Coach asked.

Rick thought he detected a note of condescension, and answered as confidently as possible. "Phone Calls, Events & Seminars and One-on-One Meetings."

"Yes, you need 80% of your work time to be on the phone or in front of people," Coach explained. "The only way to ensure you are spending enough time in the Influential Zone is to plan for it by blocking your time on an hourly basis."

"So like school? Chemistry first period, math second, and all that?" Rick asked.

"Very similar," Coach answered. "In this case, you have three courses that are going to take 80% of your workday. Stay in the Influential Zone for the majority of your time and your business will flourish.

"Schedule your Reply Times to return phone calls and check e-mail first. You're doing those at 11:00 and 4:00 right now and that's fine. Next, block off an hour of White Space a day."

"White Space?" Rick asked.

"Open time," Coach explained. "This allows you to do anything you want—catch up on paperwork, take a walk, return extra calls, grab a cup of coffee and so on. It gives you flexibility within structure.

"Also, you'll need at least four hours each week for focused phone calls to people in your Community. These times are called your Hour of Power. These are calls to the people in your database—those you've worked with in the past, networking contacts, friends, family, anybody you don't have to call, but should. Then you'll have the 1st & 10 calls. You do these as soon as you get to the office each day."

"So the people that I'm showing houses to that week?" Rick asked.

"Yes, but others as well. These calls are first thing in the morning, no exceptions. The busier you get, the more important these calls become. You'll call referral sources, cooperating agents, recent networking contacts, team members, potential clients, and so on. You'll write down the people, numbers, and reasons for your 1st & 10 calls during your Pre-Leave Ritual."

"Pre-Leave Ritual?" Rick asked. All this new terminology sounded strange.

THE FOUR ENRICHING RITUALS

"There are four rituals you are going to establish in your life as part of this coaching," Coach explained. "The greatest thing about our line of work can also be our Achilles' heel: our time is our own. These four rituals will prevent your life from getting out of control, no matter how busy you get."

"Sounds good," Rick said, still unconvinced.

"The first is your Morning Ritual. This should include your affirmations, your Blessings Book, personal preparation, and exercise. Take your morning run, lift weights, or whatever it is you do."

"Got it," Rick answered, writing it down.

"Next is the Pre-Leave Ritual I just mentioned. This is right before you leave work. Get your desk in order, write down your 1st & 10 calls, and send me your ranking on your time block for the day while you're being coached."

"So my desk should be empty?" Rick asked.

"Not necessarily. Everything just needs to be neat and set out the way you need it for the next day," Coach explained. "Third is your Pre-Sleep ritual. We all know that kids do better with a bedtime routine, but believe it or not it works on adults too. Include some reading and visualization for the next day. Some clients pray, do yoga, stretch or meditate. That's up to you, but I promise once you start you'll notice the difference in the morning."

"Okay, so what's number four?" Rick asked, realizing that they had covered the entire day.

"The fourth is your Sunday Night Ritual. You take a look at the entire week's schedule, make sure your appointments are in order and then make sure your clothes fit with the weather and what you have going on. Arrange them in the closet, right down to the socks. Some people also plan their weekly menu, but you can just start with your wardrobe. This only takes a few minutes, but it can save valuable amounts of time and energy."

"I can see that," Rick said. He was thinking about what a major adjustment even attempting to implement the Sunday Night Ritual would be.

THE NETWORKING STACK & CREATING A HOME COURT ADVANTAGE

"Now, you know my good friend Michelle, don't you?" Coach asked. Rick was startled; he half expected Coach to come out with something along the lines of *"What do you want with my daughter?"*

"Sure," he answered, a little tentatively. *Of all people to double book.*

"Of course you do," Coach chuckled. "She's the one that referred you to me. Anyway you first met her at a restaurant called EVT right there off the highway, right?"

"Yeah, how'd you know?" Rick was surprised. Coach ignored the question.

"And everyone seemed to know her, right? Hostess, waitresses, managers . . ."

"Yeah, were you there?" Rick laughed, a little sarcastically, despite himself.

"Of course not." Rick felt like a child being corrected by the principal of his school. "But the response you saw did not come because Michelle won the Miss Congeniality Award in high school. I couldn't even hear her on the phone for half of our first call. I thought I needed a hearing aid!" Rick was unable to suppress a snort. "But EVT is part of her strategy. What you observed that day is what happens when you make a restaurant your home territory. The way the staff handled her: it made you respect her and trust her more didn't it?"

"Yeah," Rick admitted.

"Now you can imagine how many referrals she's gotten from the staff there: I think it was over a dozen—direct and indirect—last time we counted and that was a few months ago. But it's not just that. It's a great way to make your networking more efficient."

"Yeah. So what do I do, go in there and act like a big shot?" Rick joked.

"Cockamamie! Rick, my hair's already gray, okay? You go in and you become a regular. Tip well. I mean 20% minimum. Get to know the staff; treat them like VIPs. Ask them about their kids, jobs, and hobbies. Remember FROG."

"Frog?" Rick asked.

"Yes, F, R, O, G, is an acronym to remind you to focus on the other person and what kind of questions to ask. Ask questions about their Family, Recreation, Occupation and Goals," Coach answered.

Rick remembered how Michelle had commented about the hostess's son and the waitress's career ambitions.

"Before you know it, it's like that show, *Cheers*, where everybody knows your name." *Yeah, it was kind of like that. I wonder if Michelle would mind if I hung out at EVT Restaurant too . . .*

"Okay, as you get to know everyone at the restaurant, and it needs to be as nice as EVT, then you start to stack your appointments one right after another. You'll have a networking lunch, and then each hour thereafter for two or three hours will be networking meetings at the same restaurant. Instead of trying to fit it in all during the week, you get it done in one day or even one afternoon." Rick remembered how many people Michelle had met that day at EVT Restaurant.

"Yeah, I'll have to get on that," Rick agreed.

"Do it now," Coach commanded. "The Networking Stack at a regular place cuts down on transportation time, you'll never be late, and you'll never get lost. Eventually, if you keep tipping well enough, you'll have home court advantage at every appointment. You could spend a lot of money and join a private club, but some contacts might not feel comfortable meeting you there. This offers you a neutral location with all those advantages and none of the costs.

"Also, you can strategically schedule people to help your business and their businesses. Remember, the person you meet at 1 p.m. meets your 11:30 A.M. *and* your 2 P.M., and the connector you meet at 2 P.M. gets introduced to the people who you meet at 1 P.M. and 3 P.M. Strategically schedule Ambassadors and Connectors next to a potential client or somebody that could help his business. The Networking Stack at a classy restaurant is a critical strategy for growing and nurturing your Community."

"Okay, I'm going to give it a try."

"Cockamamie! Look, Rick, in Basic Training they don't tell you to try to get over the wall, and this is your Basic. There is no try. There's only do. Think of it as starting an exercise regimen. Everything is hard and hurts at first, but you'll reap the benefits if you stick with it. Focus on one thing at a time: this multitasking business is overrated."

"Yeah, I guess so." Rick laughed.

"I can tell this is going to be a challenge for you. So I want you to turn in your two-week time block[9] to me by midnight tonight. I'll be up."

"It'll be there," Rick answered firmly. He knew there was no point in trying to reason with Coach about the deadline. "Gotta 'Do It Now', right?" Rick tapped the band on his wrist.

CONNECTING WITH CONNECTORS

"Exactly!" Coach said. "Okay, the next strategy is called 'Connecting with Connectors.' This is how you get ready for a networking event. Obviously, you'll learn to be strategic about picking what you attend. Now how are you going to know what to expect?"

"Check out the website for the event?" Rick ventured.

"Sure, but you're only going to check that out to find the number of whoever is in charge of membership so you can call him or her to find out what you need to know. You will ask the chairperson two questions: Find out if the introductions will be formal or informal, and the names of the top three or four people you should meet—the most influential people. Ask to be introduced to them. Got that?"

"Yeah," Rick said, jotting it down.

"Next, use that information to prepare: Google those folks so you know what to say to them. Once we're at the day of the event, what are you supposed to be thinking about?"

---

9. For examples and a blank time block worksheet, go to www.ReferralLibrary.com.

"Not sure."

"First, go with the spirit of helpfulness. Yes, you want to get business. But people can smell a taker a mile away, and it don't smell pretty, you know what I mean? Jay says to 'Lead with the giving hand' and I think that says it pretty well. Now when are you going to get there?"

"Ten minutes early?"

"Try thirty! Wear your name badge on your right side so that when you shake hands it is thrust forward and easy to read. That meeting organizer is like your compass in the wilderness: he or she will point you where you need to go. Introduce yourself to him and remind him of what he promised you. When he starts to get busy, don't pester him. Just remind him real politely, 'You had mentioned I should meet so-and-so.' You'll get your introduction."

Rick thought about a function he had attended a couple years back where he had waited for hours to meet one of the county chairpersons, only to see her chatting with Don for hours. *I wish I'd thought of this then . . .*

"Next, use FROG, just like in the restaurant, to take a genuine interest in these folks. But I think you're pretty good at connecting with people when you try . . ." Rick smiled to himself. It was nice to have a strength noticed. "And last, but certainly not least, is your follow-up strategy. Any guesses?"

"POWER Notes to everyone I meet?"

"You bet. Now notice how the Connecting with Connectors[10] strategy works with your Networking Stack. You'll meet the Connectors at the events and funnel them to your Networking Stack. Remember if people see you with the movers and shakers, they assume you are one too," Coach said matter-of-factly.

"That makes sense," Rick replied.

---

10. For the 7 Steps to Connecting with Connectors, see Glossary.

A SUCCESSFUL SUCCESS STORY

Coach shifted gears. "When was the last time you made something good happen for a client?" he asked.

Rick was silent for a moment, thinking. "Well, several months ago I did help a man unload his house. He needed to move to take care of his dad. It felt good to help him do that."

"Great. You're going to have a lot more stories like that one, but one of your action items from today will be to write me twelve success stories. Take your last twelve closings and write me a story about that client. The process is really simple.

Rick wrote:

THE 7 STEPS TO A SUCCESSFUL SUCCESS STORY:

1. *WHAT WAS THE CLIENT'S NAME AND SITUATION? (BE SPECIFIC ABOUT THE PROBLEM OR CHALLENGE.) FOR EXAMPLE: JOSH AND JILL WERE FIRST TIME HOME BUYERS.*

2. *WHAT WOULD HAVE HAPPENED IF YOU WEREN'T INVOLVED? (WHAT IS THE WORST POSSIBLE THING THAT COULD HAVE HAPPENED?) JOSH AND JILL COULD HAVE BOUGHT THE FIRST HOME THEY SAW - BACKED TO HIGHWAY.*

3. *HOW DID YOU HELP THEM SOLVE THE PROBLEM? EDUCATED THEM ON WHAT MAKES A GOOD INVESTMENT.*

4. *WHAT WAS THE RESULT? BE SPECIFIC. THEY BOUGHT A GREAT HOME THAT IS A GREAT INVESTMENT. ON CUL-DE-SAC, DESIRABLE PLAN, AND NEIGHBORHOOD THAT HAS A GOOD HISTORY OF APPRECIATION.*

5. *WHAT DID THE CLIENT SAY OR DO TO LET YOU KNOW YOU DID WELL? (INCLUDE THEIR TESTIMONIAL OR THAT THEY REFERRED ME. FOR EXAMPLE, THEY REFERRED ME TO CHRIS HILLS, ANOTHER FIRST TIME HOME BUYER.)*

6. Ask for SPECIFIC and RLLEVANT Referrals Example: Who is a person You know buying their first home – could be a renter or even a son or daughter of someone You know?

7. Call to Action. Use a sentence like: "Please reply to this e-mail with the name and their situation. I promise they'll get the excellent service they deserve."

"You have plenty to do," Coach said in an understatement. "This is a pivotal time for you and your career. After implementing the secrets in this session and studying Dan Kennedy, Stephen Covey and Brian Tracy, you're going to see a tremendous increase in your productivity."

Rick hung up the phone and stared at a blank sheet of legal paper.

All he could think about was how he was going to get his time blocking for the next two weeks done before midnight. He noticed Michelle had called. Hopeful, he checked his messages . . .

YOU'RE IN THE PEOPLE BUSINESS

5

"Love cures people – both the ones who give it and the ones who receive it."

DR. KARL MENNINGER

"HI, LISA," Rick smiled as he strode into the office. It was 8:55 A.M.

"Hey, Rick!" the receptionist answered. "In early again. You look great. Have you lost weight?"

"Trying," Rick said, secretly pleased. "I'm finally getting back in the gym and even running some."

"Well, I left your messages on your desk; there were quite a few. I guess it's true . . ." her voice trailed off as if she had let the last words slip out accidentally.

"What's true?" Rick asked, lowering his voice.

"Well, at the administrative meetings I thought I overheard that you're on pace to outsell Don this month," she whispered.

"What?" Rick was shocked. Sure business had picked up, but Don was untouchable. Rick had seen a local bus with Don's huge smiling picture just on the way to work that morning. "I thought he just sold some place to the former governor or something."

"Yeah, but I think he did that at a deep discount to get the deal. The firm hardly made any money, and besides that was last month. Oh my gosh! Don't tell anyone I said that," she added quietly.

"Don't worry," Rick assured her. "By the way, how was Mary's track meet on Saturday?"

"Oh, really great!" she answered, her eyes shining with pride. "She took second in long jump and made the finals in the open 400; there were clubs there from all over the county. Thanks for asking!"

"Well, tell her I said, 'Good job' and that she'd better give me an autograph before she goes to the Olympics." Lisa laughed as Rick went to the conference room, closed the door, and put his mobile phone on vibrate.

One by one he hammered his 1st & 10 calls out. Coach was right: it did go faster when you just sat down and concentrated on it. He enjoyed these calls and he was really enjoying the structure of the time-blocked schedule. *No more double booking for me!*

Although he had plenty of blessings to write down in his notebook each morning, Rick was still trying to recover from the disaster with Michelle. She had returned his voicemail with one of her own; it was polite enough, but Rick had a feeling she was not happy at all. He sighed heavily. He looked at the clock: *almost time to go get some coffee.*

"Hey, buddy!" Don's overly friendly, slightly condescending voice caught Rick off guard as he filled his mug.

"Hey, man," he returned, looking over his shoulder to see Dial Don himself, decked out as usual in an Italian suit and perfectly coifed hair. *I wonder if he gets manicures . . .* Rick tried to shoot a glance at Don's hands without being noticed.

"So I hear you went to that Generation Lovefest seminar when it was in town. Trying to be one of those lovey-dovey agents, huh?" *He's mocking me. I didn't know he'd heard of the Generosity Generation.*

"Yeah, I went to check it out," Rick answered trying to sound nonchalant. "Some helpful stuff, actually."

"Yeah, right!" Don laughed. "Look, I gotta tell you, I got your voicemail the other day. I was calling to see if you wanted to come to one of my open houses; I have like twenty going on but I don't know what your clients can afford. Anyway, I don't know what they told you at that seminar but that is the longest, most hilarious voicemail greeting I have ever heard in my life. You must be just hanging onto the bottom rung, right now buddy."

Rick didn't answer. Before he could think of a clever retort, Don was down the hall, offering a "Hey, buddy," to all who passed. Rick was smarting from the insult, but forced himself to focus on the tasks at hand. He had a full day ahead and another call with Coach that night.

IT'S ALL ABOUT PEOPLE

That evening Rick was close to home, his large dinner salad resting on the passenger seat of his car as he pondered the remainder of his day. He would eat, shower and be ready for his call with Coach at 9:00. He had successfully pushed the unpleasant interaction of that morning to the back of his mind until he passed Don's billboard, smiling at him from the highway exit. Like a wave, the anger and frustration hit him all over again. This was no frame of mind for a coaching call: he would have to try to pull it together somehow.

"How's the e-mail addiction?" Coach laughed, when they got started. He seemed to be in a particularly good mood.

"Oh, I think I'm almost cured," Rick said, chuckling despite the irritation that the shower had failed to wash away. "I mean, I'm too busy. Three times a day is all I can work in."

"Well I noticed your replies were coming at regular times. That's good work. Most guys take longer to kick the habit, especially with these smart phones," Coach said approvingly. "So how did the networking event go?"

"Actually, pretty well. The member chair for the Chamber of Commerce was surprisingly helpful and he did introduce me to some key people there like you said he would. Honestly, I would have been intimidated by people like this a few years ago. One is my age, the son of a former US Senator who grew up around here. I'm pretty sure I bagged groceries for his family while he was away at prep school. But I just asked him about his family and interests. Turns out, he's a huge Cowboys fan. After I found that out, we really hit it off."

"That sounds like it went really well," Coach said. Rick told him about the rest of his conversations with the influencers he had met and how he had used FROG to break the ice, keep the focus on the Connectors and retain control of the dialogue. "Good job, Rick. I'm proud of you. Now are you ready for the Magic Question?"

"I guess so," Rick said, wondering what that could possibly mean.

THE MAGIC QUESTION & THE DISCOVERY

"Okay, here we go: How would your best friend describe you: 1) straight-to-the-point, 2) social and outgoing, 3) steady and dependable, or 4) cautious and perfectly accurate?"

"I'm a little bit of all those Coach," Rick replied.

"If you had to just choose one, which would it be?"

"I would say I'm straight-to-the-point," Rick answered.

"Me too," Coach said. "Rick, I want you to put the Magic Question on all your intake forms and next to your phone. You'll learn how important it is to know the behavioral style of your client. There are four distinct behavioral styles. Everybody has some of each, but one of them is typically more dominant than the others. The four behavioral styles spell the acronym DiSC.®[11]

"D stands for Dominance. D's are straight-to-the-point. They tend to be driven, fast-paced, impatient, efficient and brutally honest. They aren't into long explanations: they want the bottom-line."

"Got it," Rick said, jotting it down. *That's me, all right.*

"I stands for Influence, and i's love socializing. They are often outgoing, friendly, emotional, and energetic. They're the life of the party." *Just like my sister, and half the waitresses at EVT . . .*

"S is Steadiness. An S is steady and dependable," Coach continued. "S's nurture. They live to serve and please others. They prefer predictability and security over spontaneity and excitement. They enjoy executing systems." *Sounds like Michelle.* Rick was surprised how naturally everyone's behavior seemed to fit into these categories that Coach was describing.

"C is for Compliance. C's are perfectionists who expect everyone to comply with the rules. These guys crave order and process. They can seem almost inflexible. This is the person that tells you, 'It's more important to do it right than to do it fast.'" Rick laughed, thinking of his old friends at the accounting firm. He thought he remembered a consultant doing something with behavioral styles there.

"Pretty interesting stuff, Coach," Rick said thoughtfully. "I guess we D's rule the world?"

"Well, we'd like to," Coach said. Rick detected the hint of a smile. "But that's not how it works. There's no right or wrong

---

11. DiSC® is a registered trademark of Inscape Publishing. Used with permission. All rights reserved. Please see www.EverythingDiSC.com for more information.

way to be. It's recognizing your strengths and weaknesses. Remember to be alert to your clients' behaviors and the fact that the buying process tends to bring out everyone's inner C."

"Inner C?" Rick asked.

"The bigger the purchase, the more attention to the details. In life, there are three things that you should never mess with a person about: his family, his home and his money. The interesting thing about your profession is that you get to mess with all three at the same time. People are going to want details, specifics and facts," Coach explained.

"Yeah, that makes sense. So many times as an agent, it's easy to wonder what people get so worked up about. But it's the largest amount of money most of them will ever spend," Rick thought out loud.

"Now you're getting it," Coach affirmed. "Listen, have you heard of the Platinum Rule?"

Well, Don told me the golden rule means that the one with the most gold makes the rules. "I remember the Golden Rule is to treat others as you'd want to be treated. I do remember Jay said something about the Platinum Rule, but I can't remember what it was," Rick admitted.

"Cockamamie! Rick, this is important!" Coach reprimanded. "It means you're supposed to treat people the way THEY want to be treated, even if it's not what you would want yourself."[12]

"Sell the way the buyer buys?"

"Exactly," said Coach. "Here's a short poem to remind you how to treat everybody:

---

12. Dr. Tony Alessandra and Dr. Michael J. O'Connor wrote *The Platinum Rule* which covers this concept and much more. Please see www.ThePlatinumRule.com for more information.

> The DiSCovery
>
> Care like Everyone's an S,
> Smile like Everyone's an i,
> Prepare like Everyone's a C,
> & Sell like Everyone's a D.

"I want you to type this up and put it in your office."

"Cool," Rick complimented.

"Now this is just a quick introduction. You need to make sure that you know these categories inside and out. Let's see how well you know them with a little test."

"Okay," Rick agreed, trying not to betray his mild anxiety.

"I'm your client, James. You've figured out that I'm a D. Leave me a voicemail telling me you found my house."

After a few moments of thought, Rick replied, "Hi, this is Rick Masters. I just wanted to let you know that I found a home for you that matches the criteria you gave me. It has four bedrooms, three and a half bathrooms, and it even has that three-car garage you were looking for. Please call me as soon as you can. Thank you."

"That's not bad, Rick. Not bad for being put on the spot. But it needs to be shorter. A D doesn't want to hear all that."

He's right. Rick thought of Don mocking his voicemail and realized that some clients were the type who didn't want to listen to more than they had to. He tried again. "Hi James, this is Rick. I found it. Give me a call as soon as you get this.'"

"Much better," Coach said. "How about for an i?"

Rick didn't hesitate. "Hi James! This is Rick. Hey buddy, I've got that home you've been looking for. It's got a huge kitchen and back deck for your famous parties. It's just down the road from your favorite professional baseball player as well. Ring me when you get a minute."

"Good," Coach said approvingly. "I think you're getting this. How about the S? Remember to slow your delivery down for the S's."

Rick paused briefly. "Hi James. Rick here. Hope your day is going well. Wanted to let you know I've been working for you. I found a home for you. It's on a cul-de-sac. Safe and sound for the family. Also wanted to let you know that the family who is selling it is very nice and have been great to work with so far. Can you round up the troops for a showing tomorrow afternoon? Schedule it for 2:00 on the family calendar and let's get together." Rick thought he might have been overdoing and waited to see what Coach would say.

"Very good Rick," Coach said. "That was your best yet. Appealing to family, safety, and showing sensitivity to the calendar was well done. Now let's go for the C."

Rick shuddered, imagining life back at the accounting firm, and said crisply, "Hi James, Rick Masters here. It's 12:35 and I located a house at 123 Anywhere Street. It has four bedrooms, three bathrooms, and a three-car garage. It's 3551 square feet and price-wise fits in the lower half of the neighborhood. I can show you tomorrow at 2:00 P.M. but we'll have to be done by 3:30 P.M. Please call me between 1:00 and 4:00 today to let me know you have received this and want to see the home. Thank you."

"Great!" Coach said, despite himself. "For a D, you really get this. You've got some more reading on the topic, but I think we can move on to One-on-One Meetings." Rick was pleased. This was the first unqualified praise he remembered hearing from Coach.

ONE-ON-ONE MEETINGS

"Now, you'll remember that One-on-One Meetings are at the top of the Communication Pyramid. These are the most important hours of your week, so you need to prepare for them."

Coach continued his instruction, explaining how Rick would create a Spectrum of Solutions[13] like Michelle's, a brochure that would help him show his clients what he had to offer rather than giving them a long speech. He would be able to focus on learning about them and their businesses rather than explaining what he had to offer.

"Start by doing Internet research on the people you're meeting and taking the Spectrum of Solutions. Once you're there, remember these four things. First, remember FROG. This is about them, not you. Ask about their family, recreation, occupation and goals.

"Second, and this goes along with goals, ask them what their biggest challenges are right now. You're there to help, so you need to know what they need. Third, match their natural pace of conversation. The fast talkers will be an easy fit for you. Just make sure you take cues from the ones who're a little more deliberate, and slow it down a bit."

"And fourth?" Rick asked.

"End your One-on-One Meetings with one or both of these questions: how can I help you and what can I do for you?" Coach said seriously. "Your action item for every One-on-One is to leave with an assignment that you will get done by the end of that day."

"And a POWER Note to follow-up, right?" Rick asked eagerly.

"A POWER Note, of course," Coach said matter-of-factly.

"But now we need to talk about the F-Bomb," Coach said seriously.

"What?" Rick asked. *What is he talking about?*

---

13. For an example of a Spectrum of Solutions, please go to www.ReferralLibrary.com.

"In Seven Levels, the f-word is follow-up," Coach explained. "The F-Bomb is a system for follow-up that you'll create for your One-on-One Meetings: a seven week series of POWER notes, direct mail pieces, e-mails, and phone calls. At least four of your follow-up touches need to be phone calls. Use your CRM or calendar to schedule these tasks to take place."

"Should I use my Success Stories for the direct mail pieces and e-mails?" Rick asked. "Also, should I take a gift to these meetings?"

"Affirmative on both," Coach answered quickly. "A relevant book can make a great gift. But more important is preparing for One-on-Ones by watching great interviewers such as Barbara Walters and Roy Firestone. You'll also read Daniel Goleman's *Social Intelligence* and listen to Dale Carnegie's classic, *How to Win Friends and Influence People*, which will help you get the most out of these meetings."

"Got it," Rick said, jotting down the resources.

"Now I want to wrap up by talking about the power of words. In the Seven Levels, we never ask directly for referrals."

"What? I thought that's what this was all about?" Rick asked, taken aback.

"You've already seen that you're going to get plenty of referrals, but you're never going to say to someone 'please refer me to your friends and family,'" Coach clarified. "Instead you're going to ask people to either introduce you to those they love and trust—neighbors, friends, family members and co-workers—or to be connected to influencers and other connectors."

"Okay," Rick said, unsure of the difference.

"Listen," Coach explained. "A referral is like an emotionally-charged endorsement; someone puts his reputation on the line for you. It's easier for a person to introduce you to a friend than refer you. A connection is just what it sounds like: someone putting you in touch with an individual you should meet. Now it's okay to explain your business philosophy using the word 'referral.' But asking for a referral can make people unnecessarily uncomfortable. Does that make sense?"

"Now it does," Rick replied. With that, Rick realized their time was almost up.

LESSON LEARNED

"So we've got a couple of minutes," Coach said. "You want to tell me what had you so bothered at the beginning of this call?"

Rick bristled. "Well, it's really stupid," he faltered, wondering how obvious it had been that he was upset.

"All the more reason to get over it," Coach pointed out.

"Yeah, I guess you're right," Rick agreed, and he recounted briefly his little interaction with Don. To his dismay, Coach burst out laughing.

"That's the funniest thing I've heard in a while, Rick," Coach laughed a hearty, deep laugh. He was barely able to contain himself.

"Glad to entertain you," Rick said, slipping back into his old sarcasm.

"No," Coach laughed. "Don't you see? Don is threatened by you. That's why he's running you down!"

"What?" Rick was truly shocked. The possibility had never occurred to him.

"Sure. When you were in the doldrums, did Don ever speak to you?"

"Well, not much," Rick admitted. "I mean, he'd say hi once in a while, and he told me he thought I'd be out of business in a year when I asked if he would help me . . ." Rick remembered with embarrassment his desperate request to Don for leads, ideas, or anything to get his business out of the gutter.

"Of course he didn't. You weren't on his radar. Now didn't you say that the receptionist hinted you might have been close to his numbers this month?"

"Well, yeah, I guess. But I don't see how that can be right . . ." Rick trailed off.

"Well, if he's doing high profile deals for cut rates like she seemed to think, you probably are nipping at his heels. That's why he called you to come to his open houses and that's why he took time out of his busy day to come and insult you in the break room. Rick, think about it."

Rick thought about it. As angry as he had felt, Coach's take on this situation made a lot more sense.

"Now, what about your housewarming parties? You set up that appointment with Michelle like we'd discussed by e-mail?" Rick's heart sank again. He swallowed hard.

"The truth is, I'm afraid Michelle's mad at me."

"What'd you do to make Michelle mad?" Coach sounded like a protective dad again.

"Well, I double booked an appointment with a client at the time I was supposed to meet her for lunch. I really would have rather met with her, but I had to go with the client, you know? I promise you, since I've been time blocking, I haven't double booked once."

"Gotcha. Well, my guess is that Michelle's not as much mad as she is hurt. She let you into her circle, tried to help you out and you're kind of saying that you don't really value what she's offering you."

But that's exactly the opposite of how I feel! Rick thought in frustration.

"There's not much you can do but come clean. Have you tried calling her?" Coach asked.

"Yeah, I left a voicemail and she returned it with another. She didn't sound mad but she didn't sound happy either," Rick explained.

"Well, call her again and this time, leave her a voicemail for an S with a real apology. We all make mistakes, Rick. It's bound to happen sooner or later. The only thing you can do is own up to it and ask for forgiveness."

Coach assigned Rick his action items and they said their goodbyes.

THE APOLOGY

Rick found himself staring at the wall for a minute or so. He knew what he had to do, but he couldn't think of how to do it. How could he express how sorry he was to Michelle without making it sound corny or fake? What would Coach do?

Rick jumped up from the table and ran to his office to retrieve a legal pad. Of course! Pad and pen in hand, he drafted various wordings until he was sure he had it just right. Finally he was ready to call. If she answered, great. If not, he was prepared. He tapped the band on his wrist and dialed.

"Michelle, this is Rick. I want you to know that I am truly sorry for having to cancel our appointment the other day. I want you to know that I appreciate everything you've done for me since we met. You've gone out of your way to introduce me to people who have so much to offer me, especially Coach. You were right, he has grown on me. Anyway, I hope we can meet sometime soon. Let me know when your schedule is free. No double-booking this time, I promise!"

PHONE CALLS

6

"Too often we underestimate the power of a touch, a smile, a kind word, a listening ear, an honest compliment, or the smallest act of caring, all of which have the potential to turn a life around."

LEO BUSCAGLIA

RICK OPENED HIS EYES and tried to focus on the clock. It was 4:30 A.M. and he had been tossing and turning for an hour. He rubbed his eyes; his skin felt moist and hot. The flu? It was that time of year. He reached for the bottle of water by his bedside and took a drink. His throat felt raw. *Not now! I have too much to do tomorrow.*

Rick's head pounded as he dragged himself to the bathroom to look in his medicine cabinet. *This is so weird . . . I've been eating healthy, working out, feeling great. I've got so many appointments today . . .* Rick's thoughts continued in a blur as he found some cold medicine. He closed the cabinet door, looked at himself in the mirror, and shook his head. Then it hit him: *Success Suicide! Of course!* This was the breakdown before the breakthrough Coach was talking about it!

He had achieved almost everything he wanted and his body had picked this moment to succumb to a virus. Well, it didn't matter. He would do exactly what Coach said to do: he would persevere. Rick took the medicine, chased it with some water, checked to make sure his alarm was set and went back to bed.

GET UP, GET GOING, GET A REFERRAL

Rick hung up the phone and checked his watch. Right on time: he had just spent an hour following up on self-appointed action items and he needed to leave in the next ten minutes to get to EVT Restaurant. He pulled into the parking lot and waited for the CD in his car to finish. Of course this was *How to Win Friends and Influence People,* which Coach had assigned to him. Rick found he didn't miss his other educational materials that much.

"Hi Rick!" Katherine said, smiling at him from behind the hostess stand, "Good to see you again! Same table?"

"Absolutely," Rick smiled back. It was hard to believe he had never been to this place a couple of months ago. Katherine ushered him to his table and just as he was sitting down, he caught a glimpse of a familiar face in the lobby.

"Michelle!" Katherine and Michelle shared their customary embrace and Rick stood to intercept them as they headed to Michelle's regular booth.

Both women smiled and Michelle extended her hand warmly and said, "Hi, Rick! I got your voicemail. Thanks so much." Katherine left the menus on Michelle's table and excused herself to go back to her post.

"I promise that will never happen again. Will you ever forgive me?" Rick asked, surprised to hear his sheepish tone.

"Of course!" Michelle said warmly. "So you're enjoying Coach?"

"Yes, I'm learning to," Rick laughed, glad to be in Michelle's good graces again. "He's tough like you warned me, but I'm starting to think he's just what the doctor ordered."

"I'm so glad," Michelle said, giving his arm an affectionate squeeze. "Well, I know you're here for appointments and so am I, so I'll call you and we'll set up that time to talk about the housewarming parties, okay?"

"Sounds great!" Rick smiled. Katherine was escorting the builder he was meeting, but over his shoulder he could see Alan in the lobby. *That must be her lunch date.*

"Hi there!" Rick smiled, rising to shake Jerry's hand.

"Hey, Rick. Nice spot! Listen, I gotta run to the restroom real quick. Remind me to tell you about Jim. He's a buyer. Order me a coffee, okay?" Jerry departed and Rick found himself straining to see if he could hear anything going on at Michelle's table. He couldn't, but he noticed that they had the same waitress as he did today.

"Hi, Theresa," Rick said as she made her way to his table after taking Alan and Michelle's drink order.

"Hi, Rick," she smiled. "What can I get you guys to drink?"

"Hot tea with lemon and honey for me and coffee for my friend." Rick felt better, but his throat was still a little sore. "How's Bailey's foot?"

"Oh, the vet fixed it right up! Thanks for asking. You see Alan come in to meet Michelle?" she asked. Rick detected a note of disapproval. He looked up at her.

"Oh did he?" Rick asked casually. *Did Theresa just smirk at me?*

"Yeah, I just don't know about him for her, you know?"

"What do you mean?" Rick asked, trying not to sound too interested.

"I don't know. Michelle's such a sweetie . . ." But before Theresa could finish, Jerry was back at the table, and she left to retrieve their drinks.

IS IT GOOD TO HEAR FROM YOU?

"Hello. Coach speaking," Coach answered in his gruff voice.

"Hi Coach!" Rick said cheerfully.

"Well, someone's been doing his affirmations," Coach laughed.

"Yeah, I have to admit they're not a waste of time like I first thought," Rick confessed.

"Well it all works together. No one wants to be around a grump, as my dad used to say. People want to feel good about themselves and the better you feel, the better you can make them feel. The more you actually care, the easier it is to actually help and then the more they'll want to help you."

"Makes sense," Rick agreed.

"Okay, as you know, we're going to cover Phone Calls today. Now where does this fit in the Communication Pyramid?" Coach asked.

"It's Level Three overall, but it's the first level of the Influential Zone," Rick answered confidently.

"Good," Coach said. "Now what do you already know about Phone Calls from our sessions so far?"

"Well, I know I need to consistently block off time to give them my undivided attention. I've already started doing that and it's made a huge difference."

"Good, let's conquer what they call 'call-reluctance.' Ever feel any hesitance about your calls?" Coach asked.

"Sure, especially calling clients who closed a long time ago," Rick answered.

"Rick, if you are reluctant to call, it's really because you're being selfish."

"How so?" Rick was genuinely curious.

"If you're hesitating to call, it's because you're thinking about yourself. If you're thinking about helping the people you're calling and focusing on *their* needs, it's easy to pick up the phone." Rick thought about this in silence.

"Now after each call I want you to rank yourself."

"Rank myself?" Rick asked.

"On a 0 to 10 scale: how happy was the person to hear from you? Zero means they hung up on you and ten means it was like reconnecting with your best friend. You want people to look at the Caller-ID, see that it's you and be excited to answer the phone," Coach explained.

"The way to get people to look forward to your call is to help them," he continued. "Call with a heart to help. They may need contractors' information, the location for a vendor, a job recommendation, or whatever. You can take the time after the call to get them whatever they need. In the meantime, you're connecting them to your referral partners, strategic allies and other people who can help them. Their network grows bigger and your Community grows stronger by helping others."

"Makes sense," Rick noted. "But how do you get people to see that you're really here to help? How do I show them I'm different from the other guys?"

A MORE POWERFUL HOUR OF POWER

"Rick, that's a great question. That's the heart of what we're getting at." Coach seemed pleased. "Get away from thinking about how this person can help grow your business. If he takes the conversation there, that's great, but you want to get to know him and figure out how you can help. Your objective is to assign yourself at least one action item when it's over, just like your One-on-Ones. Focus your attention on finding something that you can do for that person by the end of that call."

"Got it!" Rick was excited. He had always struggled with what to say when the conversation wasn't headed in a particular direction: now he had a tangible goal he could work towards.

"Now remember," Coach continued. "The person who talks the most dominates the conversation, but the person who asks the questions controls the conversation. Most people will love the fact that you are interested enough to ask for more information."

"So what kind of questions would you ask?"

"Another good question," Coach said approvingly. "Besides FROG, there are two phrases that will come in handy for you; 'tell me more about that,' and 'what's important about that to you?' These two phrases allow you to go to the next level of depth in the conversation. How do you think you would use these phrases in your business?"

"Well," Rick started. "It could relate a lot to a client's reasons for buying."

"Exactly," Coach agreed. "The 1st & 10 has been getting your day started off on the right foot and the Hour of Power is getting you ahead of the game, but now we're going to look at a way to enhance both of those."

"Okay," Rick agreed.

Coach said in a serious tone, "This is the lesson that will make or break your career in the long run. For someone to buy from you, he has to trust you. That trust comes from communication. The Seven Levels is about maximizing your communication to increase trust. The more people trust you, the more people will buy from you. The faster they trust you, the sooner they'll buy."

"I see that," Rick said thoughtfully.

"Now once you've established a relationship to where you're ranking yourself at an 8 or above on that call, you're moving into the referral zone. You've probably had a couple of conversations, and you've taken action to help them out in a couple of ways. You've built their trust and now it's time to have a referral conversation."

REFERRAL CONVERSATIONS

"Okay," Rick said. He was getting a little concerned that the information was coming too fast.

"Now don't worry," Coach assured him, "I have several scripts we're going to go through, and we'll keep going through them until you get it, okay?"

"Great," Rick answered.

"We all know birds of a feather flock together so it only makes sense that folks who are buying their first homes or selling within a neighborhood know others who would be interested in doing the same thing. Name a client you helped recently," Coach said.

"David and DeAnna," Rick responded after a moment's thought. "They were referred by someone who had received one of my POWER Notes. They're first time home buyers who are now under contract to buy. They looked at quite a few and we finally found a great fit."

"What were their living arrangements before?" Coach asked.

"They were renting a townhome," Rick quickly answered.

"Okay, so how are you going to ask them for a referral without using the word 'referral'," Coach challenged him.

Rick paused and took a deep breath, "David, it's been terrific working with you and DeAnna; do you know anyone looking to buy a home soon?" Rick cringed, waiting for the cockamamie.

"Rick, not great, but you would probably get a referral out of that," Coach said approvingly, "Just a few small changes will increase your odds. Start with 'who' not 'do' and work 'is another renter or first time buyer like you' into your question."

Rick took a second. "David, it's been great working with you. Who is another renter or first time home buyer like you who is looking to buy a home soon?" *That sounded pretty good.*

"Yes," Coach said, satisfied. "More specific is better. Whatever category or niche they fit in, ask for that and it greatly increases your odds. This is a very important concept to remember. As my father would say, you don't hunt for deer in the ocean." Rick laughed.

They practiced the "who . . . like you" dialogue until Rick had it down in his own words.

"Okay, so let's work on another effective way to get referrals," Coach said. "Hi, Rick. I know how important your time is these days. I'm looking to grow my business and I want to grow my business with great people like you. Something I've found is that great people tend to know great people. So with that in mind, out of all the people you know; who is the next person you know who will be buying, selling, or investing in real estate?"

Rick took notes and took his turn practicing the script for several minutes. Coach kept having him repeat it until he knew it perfectly. They experimented with relaxing his language to make it more conversational. Rick found it quickly became natural.

"After you ask, give them time to answer. Don't be afraid of silence in the conversation," Coach advised. "Let silence help you. So many people get uncomfortable and feel compelled to say something. Don't do it!

"Now we're getting into the heart of referral country. There is actually a specific part of your clients' brains you're going to activate to help get you referrals," Coach said with more animation in his voice than Rick ever remembered hearing.

"Seriously?" Rick asked. "Is this like affirmations—sending them subconscious messages to find me referrals?"

"It's a little different," Coach chuckled. "Let me ask you this. When you bought your BMW, did you start to notice other BMWs on the road?"

"Yeah," Rick laughed. "I did. I would see them everywhere. Now I just see the new ones!"

"Okay, well that's an example of a particular part of your brain—your Reticular Activating System or RAS—at work. The RAS controls what you focus on; it's what enables you to pick out your son's voice calling for you in a crowd . . . or pick out a BMW when there are dozens of other cars on the road. This is the part of your clients' brains you want to put to work for you."

"How?" Rick asked. Something in the way Coach said "son" tugged at Rick's heart.

"Pretty simple. You say something along the lines of, 'Mr. and Mrs. Client, now that you are buying a house you have Supersonic Hearing and X-Ray Vision for real estate. You're going to notice that dozens of people around you are buying, selling, or investing. I ask that when you see, hear, or meet a person who mentions real estate, you give them my card and give me a call. My promise to you is that I will respond quickly to determine how I can help them. Would you do that for me please?'"

"Wow," Rick said, thinking it over. "So then, assuming they say yes, I would give them some cards?"

"Exactly," Coach said. Rick thought Coach might be smiling on the other end of the phone.

"Can we go over it a few more times?" Rick asked. They practiced the RAS dialogue until Rick was completely comfortable.

THE TRIANGLE OF TRUST

"Now I want to come back to a question you asked earlier about how you convince someone that you're different than the other guy. Have you ever noticed that when somebody else speaks highly about you, it's far more convincing than when you speak highly about yourself?"

"Sure." Rick smiled remembering how back in high school Brian had told one of the cheerleaders that Rick had saved his life so Rick could ask her to Homecoming.

"Well, getting a third-party endorsement of your services can be very powerful, but in my experience most salesmen don't do what it takes to secure them. Any time you can orchestrate a third-party endorsement, do so. Look for opportunities to have somebody else sing your praises, introduce you to someone they know, or connect you to a connector. We call it the Triangle of Trust."

"Like at the networking events where I get in good with the organizer and ask him to introduce me?"

"That's exactly right," Coach answered, "but it also works with stacking your appointments. If you're having lunch with an Ambassador and a potential client, have the Ambassador speak on your behalf to the client. That makes a more powerful sales pitch than anything you'll learn in a library of books on sales and marketing. The more influential your Ambassador, the more powerful your introduction will be. And you know what they say about first impressions."

"Yeah, you're right," Rick agreed.

THE SPOKES TO HUB STRATEGY

Coach continued, "Now for the big fish, you can employ what we call the Spokes to Hub Strategy. It's like the Triangle of Trust on steroids. That's where you get several people to speak to a particular Connector on your behalf."

"Wow!" Rick exclaimed. "I'm glad you brought this up because there's a local human resources director I've been trying to run into. Her company relocates dozens of people yearly and doesn't use a relocation firm."

"Well," Coach started. "Who do you know who knows her?"

"Well, several employees are clients of mine."

"It's simple," Coach assured him. "Call three or four of them during your 1st & 10 time. Ask them if they would call her or e-mail her that day to let her know that you will be calling at 4:00 P.M. Ask them to say a couple of kind words about you and let her know that she should at least take your call. Most will agree."

"If nothing else, that's a great time to reconnect with those clients," Rick said, thinking of a couple he hadn't spoken to in a while. "Now, what do I say when I call her?"

"What do you think would be appropriate?"

"I need to start with the idea of helping her," Rick said slowly, thinking it through. "I can ask her to describe her biggest challenge to me."

"You've earned a stripe today, private," Coach answered with a laugh.

THE TRIANGLE OF TRUST AT WORK

"Now before we finish, I want to show you how all this works," Coach said. "Rick, do you have a CPA?"

"Yes," Rick answered.

"How would you rate your CPA on a scale of 1 to 10 with 1 being 'poor' and 10 being 'excellent'?"

"10, easily," Rick answered. "I worked with him at the old firm. He's saved me thousands over the years."

"Will you give me his contact information?"

"Of course. Are you going to call him? "

Coach ignored the question. "Rick, would you do me a favor? As soon as we're done with today's call and since you have his info out, will you immediately call your CPA to let him know that I will be calling him today between 4:00 and 5:00? Let him know how we know each other. Will you do that for me please?"

"Sure," Rick said. He wasn't sure where this was leading.

Coach ignored the confusion in Rick's answer and continued, "Just so you know, I am looking for a few CPAs to refer business to. I'm looking for 10s. I am going to meet with three or four and your CPA will be one of those I meet, not just for my personal business, but for the opportunity to meet people in my Community. Anything I need to know before I meet him?"

"He loves sports," Rick answered. "Especially baseball. He's a baseball history buff and knows every stat imaginable for every player. He's married and has two daughters. He's not like most CPAs in that he has an outgoing personality and does quite a bit of networking. I sold their old home."

"Great," Coach said. "Thank you. I appreciate the introduction. I'm going to let you go now. I know you're busy, but could you do me a favor and call him now?"

"Sure—" Rick looked at the clock. They still had time left on their call.

"Okay, Rick, don't hang up," Coach said gently. "What we just went through is what I want you to do with the people you respect most until you've talked to at least ten people."

"Oh," Rick said, mildly embarrassed. "So that's how you increase your Community with top quality people?"

"Not only that, but you're also getting warm introductions to these top performers," Coach added. "Plus, the client is referring you so they get a win with their CPA, financial planner, attorney, or whomever they introduce to you."

Rick thought about it for a second. "Wow, not everybody is going to rate their CPA a 10. I'd guess at least half of the calls would be with people who *needed* CPAs. You're calling and then meeting with these 10-graded CPAs with at least five referrals in your pocket. You could give one referral to each or give five to the best one."

"And why is it important to show up at each meeting with referrals in your pocket?" Coach prodded.

"Well, aside from confidence," Rick started, "you'd be going into a relationship giving referrals. That helps you get referrals too . . ."

Rick and Coach practiced the Triangle of Trust scripting a few more times using different professions in place of CPAs. A light went on in Rick's head. Michelle had used this to meet him!

THE TRIANGLE OF TRUST

MICHELLE WANTS TO MEET TOP-NOTCH, REFERABLE AGENTS. SHE JUST RE-FINANCED JOSH.

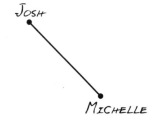

JOSH

MICHELLE

MICHELLE ASKS JOSH, "IF YOU HAD A FRIEND OR NEIGHBOR WHO WAS LOOKING TO SELL OR BUY, WHO WOULD YOU RECOMMEND TO THEM?" JOSH SAYS, "MY BUDDY RICK."

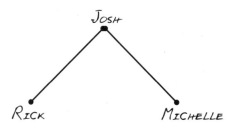

JOSH

RICK   MICHELLE

MICHELLE ASKS JOSH TO INTRODUCE HER TO RICK. JOSH AGREES TO CALL RICK (ESSENTIALLY TO WARM UP MICHELLE'S CALL). MICHELLE CALLS A FEW HOURS LATER.

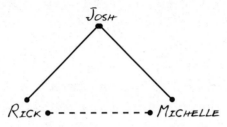

IT IS NOW UP TO MICHELLE TO DETERMINE IF RICK WOULD MAKE A
GOOD REFERRAL PARTNER.

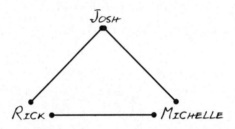

CONTRAST THIS WITH MICHELLE GOING DIRECTLY TO RICK. WITHOUT
THE ESTABLISHED WARMTH AND TRUST OF JOSH'S INTRODUCTION,
MICHELLE IS FAR LESS LIKELY TO ESTABLISH A STRONG RELATION-
SHIP WITH RICK. THIS IS ALSO A GREAT "WARM-UP" REFERRAL FOR
JOSH. MICHELLE CAN FOLLOW UP WITH JOSH LIKE HE REFERRED
RICK (WHICH HE DID, BUT IT IS A SOFT REFERRAL). THIS STRATEGY
IS CRITICAL TO GROWING YOUR COMMUNITY WITH STRONG REFERRAL
PARTNERS. IT IS COMMUNICATING WITH YOUR COMMUNITY VERSUS
MARKETING TO STRANGERS.

"Very good," Coach said. "Now I want to close with one last script. You are going to get into conversations with people who may or may not have a relationship with a real estate agent. You're going to need to be able to find out without asking directly. This is the *Are You the Chosen One* script.

ARE YOU THE CHOSEN ONE?

"Okay, I'm ready," Rick said.

"If you had a friend or neighbor who was looking to sell their home, who would you recommend they call?" Coach asked. "That's it. Instead of asking them to directly refer you, you are asking who they would recommend. The key is how you react after they tell you."

"After they tell me?" Rick asked.

"No matter what they say," Coach explained, "you need to react positively. Get out of judgment and into curiosity[14]. If they say someone else's name, you need to say something positive about that agent and ask how they know each other. Find out what they like about the other agent. If they don't know, ask them what it would take for you to be their guy. Lastly if they say you, you're obviously in great shape and should show appreciation." Rick had another flashback to his lunch with Michelle.

They were now over time, so to end the call Coach clarified Rick's action items and assigned two books, *The Fred Factor* by Mark Sanborn and *Raving Fans* by Ken Blanchard, to go along with an audio book of *The Go-Giver* by Bob Burg and John David Mann.

Rick looked over his notes, and then at the neat stacks of paperwork he had for two deals that were supposed to close next week. It felt good to be busy, but not just because he was out of his financial panic. Something else was different . . . no, a lot of things were different.

Rick's pondering was interrupted by his phone buzzing to let him know he had a voicemail. The log showed a missed call from Michelle. As tired as he was, he felt a small burst of energy. He picked it up and listened.

---

14. Thank you, Howard Brinton.

"Rick, it's Michelle. I just wanted to let you know that I'll have to leave our meeting on Friday right at 3:00. Alan and I are going away for the weekend and we need to catch a 6:00 flight. There's a seminar in New York where my parents live and my dad actually knows a bunch of the guys Alan wants to meet with. Anyway, I think we should still be able to go through everything, but if you want to get together a little earlier, let me know."

COMMUNICATION PLANS

Rick took another drink of his water and entered some more information in his database. One more name to go in his 1st & 10, and he was moving ahead of schedule. Rick was looking forward to this last call. He had been meaning to reconnect with his college friends Jason and Tammy for a long time. They had been one of his first sales when he initially switched careers. Although they might go a year without seeing one another, it always seemed like they picked up right where they left off.

"Tammy! This is Rick Masters, how are you?" he said warmly.

"Oh my gosh, I can't believe it's you! Jason and I were just talking about you last night," the cheerful voice on the other end replied.

"Really?" Rick asked.

"Well, you won't believe what we just did! Jason got promoted last year and you know how you were always telling us we would outgrow this house when the boys got bigger? Well we just bought a new place across town—huge yard for the kids and a great finished basement. We're moving next week!"

"Wow . . ." Rick was speechless as he felt the blood rush out of his face. He knew he had to stay positive at all costs.

"Oh, and our house is on the market, so if you have a buyer or anything, you know we'd love to work with you again," Tammy added, completely oblivious to Rick's misery.

"That would be great, Tammy," Rick said, forcing his disappointment to the back of his mind. "I'll be sure to bring some people by. And I'd love to check out the new place too."

"Oh, you'll love it!" Tammy said. "The boys are so excited and you can all go out back and toss the football around." They chatted for another few minutes, before Tammy excused herself to go to her aerobics class. Rick hung up and sat silently for a minute. *Ouch!*

Rick quickly completed the action items from his earlier calls, locating a couple of phone numbers for clients who had requested them and e-mailing his sister so she could secure some basketball tickets for one of his contacts. He looked at his clock and decided to take his customary coffee break before his 11:30 lunch appointment.

Once again, an unwelcome voice greeted him from behind.

"Hey, Rick, how's it going, buddy?" Don's tone surprised him. It was almost pleasant.

"Hey, Don," Rick replied as he stirred in the cream. *Here we go again . . .*

"You heard I unloaded the Bancroft place, right?"

"I hadn't, but congratulations," Rick offered.

"Yeah, man. A couple of celebrities—well, actors anyway—from LA wanted some place to take their kids where no reporters could pester them. Guess they saw my bus ads . . . Anyway,

I told them this was perfect. That place is so off the beaten trail," Don laughed and flashed his million-dollar smile.

"Right," Rick agreed, forcing a small chuckle. This was really the last thing he needed right now.

"Well, anyway, my friend, if you have any big clients that can afford anything decent; you're welcome to bring them by an open house of mine. I've got a ton of properties listed in those new developments on the west side . . ." Don said as he walked out.

Ugh, that's where Jason and Tammy bought. He returned to his desk and did his best to regain some confidence. He reopened his database, noted a few updates and then, unable to concentrate, he tapped the band on his wrist and looked up Jason and Tammy's house in MLS. He found it, saw the listing agent and suppressed a groan. His stomach felt awful. He went outside to take a walk and catch some fresh air.

A FAILURE TO COMMUNICATE

"Well the first thing I want to say is, 'Good job,'" Coach said. Rick had just finished pouring out his tale of woe from the day before.

"What?" Rick had been preparing himself for at least a cockamamie or two.

"First, you were doing your 1st & 10, and that's good. Listen, Rick you're just getting started. I know I've been hard on you, but the truth is that these things can happen to anyone. I'll bet you Don's had more than his share of clients buy with someone else."

"Yeah, I doubt that," Rick said, shaking his head.

"Well, you did well," Coach said. "You kept your cool. You didn't let your feelings overpower you and make Tammy feel bad. A few months ago, my guess is you might not have had that much self-control. She's probably like most folks who have no idea how all this stuff works."

"Yeah, I think you're right. I just kept thinking that if I'd only started my 1st & 10 and Hour of Power calls a year ago, this never would have happened."

"Well, you're right about that," Coach agreed. "The good news is we're about to take all that to the next level by creating your Communication Plans."

"Well, not a moment too soon," Rick laughed. He felt better. He *had* kept his cool. Coach was right: a few months ago, he would have probably been short with Tammy and potentially ruined a fifteen-year friendship.

FROM MARKETER TO COMMUNICATOR

"So here's the deal," Coach continued. "We're working on your Communication Plan, not your Marketing Plan. You market TO someone but you communicate WITH your clients. You're going to invest in your Community the way Don invests in bill-boards and bus ads. Now, your goal is to build a Community and you build a Community by communicating. Now what's your Community of Influence?"

"I don't know," Rick answered truthfully.

"Cockamamie, Rick!" Coach exclaimed with surprise and dismay. *Ah, there it is,* Rick thought. "We've only talked about it about a thousand times. It's your database, your network. They all mean the same thing. But calling it a Community of Influence reminds you of what you're trying to do. Build a Community by staying in the Influential Zone."

"Okay, got it."

"Never forget that it's people who buy. Nothing happens until a person says, 'Yes' and no one says 'Yes' to someone he doesn't trust," Coach explained.

"And communication is how we build that trust," Rick agreed.

"Exactly. Now we start with Jay's tool called the Ultimate Memory Jogger.[15] This tool will make sure that everyone who should be in your database gets in there. Doctor, dentist, lawyer, all of them. Got it?" Coach asked. It was clear they had a lot to cover.

"Got it," Rick said.

"The next thing you're going to do is grade your database. This sounds like a big task, but you'll be surprised how fast it goes."

"Okay," Rick said. *Yeah, right.*

"Now we use five grades: A+, A, B, C and D. A+'s are your Ambassadors: these are people who refer you multiple times a year. They're like your unpaid sales staff. Anyone like that in your Community right now?"

"Well, Josh, Randy . . . and my sister," Rick said, thinking. "Does she count?"

"Absolutely. Family members can be some of the best Ambassadors you'll ever have. Now your A's are your Champions. They refer you an average of once a year," Coach explained, while Rick took notes.

"So my goal is to make my Champions into Ambassadors?" Rick asked. He thought of the referral his downstairs neighbor had given him several months ago.

"Well, not so fast. That will happen occasionally, but it's not as easy as you think," Coach cautioned.

"Why's that?"

"Well, typically, Ambassadors and Champions are different kinds of people. Ambassadors have a large network themselves and have an outgoing personality that helps them speak up about your services naturally. If a Champion is a quiet person

---

15. For the Ultimate Memory Jogger, please see www.ReferralLibrary.com.

with a small network, you're not really going to get more than one referral a year out of him, no matter what you do."

"I see," Rick mused. It was true that Josh was very involved in the local Chamber of Commerce and other networking organizations, whereas his neighbor only went out to her bridge club as far as he could tell.

"Your B's are your Potential Champions," Coach continued. "Your C's are Friends & Family. They like you and you want to stay in touch with them, but they're not necessarily sending you business. Your D's have never sent you business, nor are they going to, and they're probably people you wouldn't want referring you anyway. Remember the 'birds of a feather flock together' thing."

"Okay, so what do we do about them?" Rick asked.

"It's real simple," Coach laughed. "D means Delete. If they're D's, they don't belong in your Community. In fact, by the next session, I not only want your database graded, I want the D's gone."

PROACTIVE COMMUNICATION

"Now the biggest mistake people make is to think that communication is only something that happens spontaneously. They think you just bump into people at functions and catch up, or call when someone comes to your mind," Coach explained.

"Okay," said Rick. He wasn't sure what was so bad about being spontaneous but he resisted the temptation to ask.

"If you're going to build a successful referral based business, you have to communicate intentionally, not whenever you feel like it. You're going to develop a plan for communicating with each grade in your database. How often will you be calling them? On what days? What will be your objective when you call? By the time we're done, you'll have all that mapped out so that you'll never have to go through a Jason and Tammy situation again."

"Sounds great," Rick laughed. It felt good to laugh at a mistake . . . and know business was still coming.

"Okay, we'll start at the top: your Ambassadors deserve the most communication because they're more likely to refer you business. How often do you think you should contact your Ambassadors?"

Rick thought about it. He already spoke to Josh on a regular basis because they worked out at the same gym. He played golf with Josh and Randy and talked to his sister every week. "Well what exactly am I going to be talking about?"

"Don't worry about that right now. Let's think about a system rather than the individuals. Now, how often do you think you should contact your Ambassadors?" Coach asked again.

"Pretty often," Rick replied. "At least once per month."

"Okay, let's schedule your Ambassadors for one call per month. When are you doing your Hour of Power?" Coach asked.

"Wednesdays and Thursdays from 1:00 to 3:00," Rick replied. Quickly they figured out how he could schedule his Ambassador calls for the available segments of his Hour of Power calls, as well as scheduling them quarterly into his Networking Stack at EVT Restaurant. They talked through the details of doing a Board of Advisors meeting once Rick had more Ambassadors. He would get them all together in the same room and ask them how he can improve his service and his business.[16]

"The most important set of people you want to touch and inspire is your Community of Influence – your database contacts. You need to be communicating your solutions to your Community on a daily basis. You've decided your Ambassadors

16. For resources for your own Board of Advisors, please see www.ReferralLibrary.com.

get one call per month to set up a One-on-One soon after. Next you'll need to determine how often you'll be calling the Champions and Friends & Family groups."

"What about the Potential Champions, the B's?" Rick asked.

"We'll save those for next session. We have a little something special in store for that group," Coach said somewhat cryptically.

"Okay, so I'm actually going to plan all these calls into my calendar?"

"Yes, and you can use a recurring events feature or action plans in your CRM to make sure you communicate with each person throughout the year."

"So if Mary Parker is a Champion, and I'm going to call her four times a year, then I make sure my calendar is reminding me to call her every three months?"

"Exactly. You're going to want to make sure you have her phone number in there, or you can block all your Champion calls and Friends & Family calls together if you want. That part is up to you, as long as it's happening consistently."

"So this is actually pretty simple," Rick thought out loud. "I mean, I'm literally planning out all my phone calls for the entire year!"

"It *is* simple," Coach agreed. "But that doesn't mean everyone does it. It takes determination and tenacity to make it happen. I can't tell you how many guys I've explained this to, but only a small percentage has actually done it."

"Well, I'm going to be one of them," Rick said, surprised at the determined tone of his own voice.[17]

"Remember," Coach added, "you can create a Communication Plan for any demographic or geographic Community. That's

---

17. To see samples of Communication Plans, please go to www.ReferralLibrary.com. To learn how to create your own, ask about BOOST! Referral Mastery Training.

what Janice did with that apartment complex that she shared about at the conference."

"Yeah," Rick agreed. "She didn't know anyone's phone number or e-mail address, so she used the highest level of the Communication Pyramid available to her by using Handwritten Notes."

"You're exactly right," Coach agreed, sounding satisfied. "But, remember, the biggest bang for your buck is Phone Calls. That's where you can make a big impact on a diverse set of people in a short amount of time with the least amount of preparation."

"I see that," Rick agreed. *I'd better get the unlimited plan for my phone.*

THE SUCCESS SERIES

"One last thing," Coach said warmly, "You remember those Success Stories you've been working on so hard?"

"Sure," Rick said, trying not to roll his eyes. He had been e-mailing various edits back and forth with Coach for weeks.

"Now you're going to use all twelve. You're going to send Story 1 to everyone by e-mail this month and Story 12 to everyone by direct mail. Next month you'll e-mail Story 2 and send Story 11 on a postcard, and so on throughout the year. We call it the Success Series. Do you see how it works?"

"Yeah," Rick said, jotting it down.

"That's how you continually communicate your solutions to your Community without being overbearing or annoying. Remember, success attracts success," Coach said. "Well, we're about done. Anything else you need to ask me before we end it?"

KNOWING

"Coach, how did you know your wife was the one?" Rick blurted out. *I can't believe I just said that . . .* Rick hadn't thought about marriage since Brian's wedding eight years ago. Standing there watching Brian take his vows had only convinced Rick he wasn't ready.

"Well . . ." Coach laughed. "I'd say that's off topic, but I'm the one that said these calls would get personal. I'll give you three answers. The first thing I noticed was her smile. It's impossible to be happy with someone who's not happy, Rick. Be happy. Marry happy. And whether or not I knew that when we were both 21, I know it now. The first time she cooked for me, I knew I was in love. She had put care and love into every aspect of that meal, and I'm an old-fashioned guy: heart, stomach and all that."

"What's the third thing?" Rick asked.

"I've heard other men say this, but that doesn't make it less true for me. She makes me want to be a better man. She always has. The day I realized that was the day I took my life savings out of my mattress and went to the jeweler. You should've seen his face when I walked in with a wad of cash . . ." Coach laughed. Rick laughed too. He had no idea what Coach looked like now, let alone as a young man, but he pictured a well tanned GI in combat fatigues.

"Thanks, Coach. I appreciate you sharing that," Rick said. *Who am I? When did I become an affirmation saying, note-writing, salad eating guy who thinks about marriage?*

"Well, we all gotta grow up sooner or later. You take care, Rick," Coach said, signing off.

Rick hung up the phone and reviewed his notes, pondering Coach's words. It was time to go to the gym, but he had scheduled in an extra half-hour of free time for himself just in case. He picked up his phone and stared at it a minute before dialing.

THE NEWS

"Hello?" a friendly voice answered.

"Michelle?" Rick asked hesitantly.

"Rick!" There was a joy in her voice that made his heart leap.

"How are you?" he asked warmly.

"Oh, Rick, I can't believe it's you. You'll never believe what just happened. Alan's proposed! His whole reason for taking me to New York was to meet my parents. I'm getting married!"

"That's great!" Rick forced himself. "Congratulations."

"I know. I can't believe it!" Michelle marveled.

"Why not? He'd be crazy to let you get away," Rick said truthfully.

"Rick, you are too sweet. But me? Rick, I was in the chess club in high school, I didn't talk to anyone. Before Alan, I think I'd been out on four dates since college. After I hit 30 my parents gave up hope that they'd ever have to throw me a wedding . . . "

"Well he's very lucky," Rick said, trying desperately to cover his dismay. *Alan doesn't deserve you.*

"Honestly, I just can't believe this is happening . . . he's an attorney, and he's so successful. You should see his last girlfriend, this girl Karen. She's gorgeous . . . I just can't believe it . . . "

"Karen Wallace?" Rick asked, surprised.

"Yeah, how'd you know?" asked Michelle equally surprised.

"Oh, she's a friend," Rick said. Karen was a local attorney that Rick knew well. Sure, they had broken up over two years ago and hadn't spoken in nine or ten months. But he still considered her a friend.

"But I'm sorry, Rick." Michelle said. "You called. Is there anything I can do for you?"

"Well, I'd like to follow up on our discussion of those house-warming parties. My first one went well, but I think there are some things I need to tweak for the next few. I have some more people closing soon, and I want to make sure I don't miss the boat . . . with them," he added.

"Of course! How about Tuesday at 11:30 at EVT? We'll both be there the rest of the afternoon anyway!" she laughed.

"Sounds great," Rick said warmly. "Listen, congratulations again." They said their goodbyes. Rick rose to put on his work-out clothes which were laid out on his bed. He paused for a moment, and then took a small notebook from the drawer in his nightstand. Quickly, he turned to the W's . . .

ELECTRONIC COMMUNICATION

8

I want to share with you the best business (Twitter) tweet of all time: 'What can I do for you?' You'll be amazed at the response you get. You're in business to serve your community. Don't ever forget it."

GARY VAYNERCHUK

RICK FINISHED UP the action items from his 1st & 10 and fired up the computer for his midmorning e-mail check. Several important messages jammed his inbox and he started combing through them one by one. As he added items to his calendar he thought back to his conversation with Karen.

"Is she gorgeous?" Karen had asked. Rick had answered that she was nice looking, but not in a model or actress way. *"Then is she rich? Or is her family important? She must be ultra-successful because that's what Alan would be interested in. He's worked his way up and he's doing really well, but he's still obsessed with his image. He wants to run for office some day, trust me. That's why he needs to get married. Gotta have a wife by your side to look the part, you know?"*

Rick felt a strange combination of emotions that seemed too muddled to sort through. On the one hand, he was glad to have someone confirm what he had suspected about Alan from the first day they met at EVT Restaurant. He was glad it wasn't just

113

his imagination or masculine competitiveness. On the other hand he was distressed. Whatever thoughts he might have entertained about being with Michelle, she was his friend and the last thing he wanted was for his friend to end up with a jerk. Lastly, he was undeniably disappointed. The more he thought about Alan and Michelle together, the more uneasy he felt.

Focus Rick, he said to himself. *You'll figure out what to do about Michelle later. Focus on what you're doing now.*

He breathed a sigh of relief as he spotted an e-mail from a client that was closing at the end of the week. Rick had e-mailed the paperwork over two days ago as he traveled between showing properties. He was concerned that he hadn't heard from them yet. He opened the e-mail and sipped water.

> Thanks for your e-mail. We really appreciate all the time you took with us, but after looking over everything, Marie and I aren't sure that this is the way we want to go, so we're going to pass this time. Let us know what we need to do to get our earnest money back. Thanks again for everything.
>
> Jake

Rick was stunned. What just happened? He had lost clients before, in the old days. But not since starting the Seven Levels, unless you counted Jason and Tammy. He replayed every interaction with Jake and Marie in his head and he couldn't think of a single thing that had gone wrong. The house was in their price range, it was the perfect neighborhood, near Jake's job and their church. Rick suppressed the urge to call Jake at work that very minute.

YOU SHOULD HAVE CALLED

"Well, it sounds like this session has arrived right on time!" Coach said after listening to Rick's story.

"What do you mean?" Rick asked.

"Well, we're covering electronic communication and social media today," Coach said, as if it was obvious.

"Of course, and I'm really looking forward to it, but I'm not sure what that has to do with Jake and Marie," Rick said.

"Well you know why you lost the client, right?" Coach asked.

"No. Why?" Rick asked, genuinely puzzled.

"Because you e-mailed the paperwork! You should always do paperwork face-to-face. If that's impossible, do the next best thing and get them on the phone. I thought we talked about that a few times."

"We did, but I was showing six houses that day and I was running low on time," Rick said, faltering.

"Of course you were. Now this would have been their first house, right?"

"Yes," Rick answered.

"Well, you already know this is more money than they've ever spent in their lives. They're scared that they're making a huge mistake and then they get thirty pages of legal mumbo jumbo that make them think they're signing away the rights to their children. They panicked! And you weren't there to explain it to them. You know this is cockamamie, Rick. One of the biggest strengths of The Influential Zone is that you can listen and get feedback. You can't do that with e-mail. I wouldn't have thought I'd have to explain that to you at this point."

"No, I see what you mean."

"So you saved like what, 45 minutes by not dropping it off? Maybe an hour or two if they were real confused? Well you now know what those two hours just cost you . . ." Rick detected some compassion mixed with the disappointment in Coach's voice.

"So I guess I should never e-mail attachments, huh?" Rick asked, ashamed, but grateful that he had escaped with a single cockamamie.

"Well, no. That's not it at all. E-mail is a good tool. You've noticed by now that I use it. The key is knowing how to use it properly. A spade is good for digging up weeds but you don't want to use it to scoop ice cream!" Rick laughed in spite of himself. He was finding himself less overwhelmed and more encouraged by his coaching calls. "Now where does Electronic Communication fit in the Communication Pyramid?" Coach continued.

"In the Informational Zone," Rick responded comfortably.

"Exactly. It's at the top of the Informational Zone, but it's not in the Influential Zone. So that's your first clue as to what it's good for."

"Giving people information, right?" Rick asked.

"Yes, any time you want to inform, confirm, or attach information. Remember, an e-mail is only the promise of a future phone call," Coach pointed out.

"Yeah, I see that," Rick agreed, "and I know Jay said that you never use e-mail to sell, but can't e-mail also influence people?"

"Well of course it can. The problem is that it can easily influence people the wrong way. Ever had an e-mail backfire?"

Rick didn't have to think long. "Yeah, I sure have," he laughed. "Besides today, a few years back I wrote my girlfriend to cancel a date because I was working late. I was really brief because I was swamped and she thought I was ditching her . . ."

"And what happened?" Coach laughed.

"We got in a huge fight," Rick recalled. "It took me three dozen roses to fix that one!"

"So there you have it. It's easier to take a relationship from a 5 to a 1 than it is to take it from a 5 to 6 with e-mail. One wrong word can cost you many phone calls—or roses! As D's, we have to be even more conscientious about this.

"Once you've established a rapport with someone so that they're as likely to refer you as not, it takes a deliberate investment of time and energy to move them up that scale. Remember the Impact Arrow on the Communication Pyramid. All you have to do is send one e-mail that makes them uncomfortable or gets misinterpreted, and you're right back at the bottom."

"Okay, I'm convinced," Rick sighed. "Now what were you saying last time about the plan for the B's in my database?"

A MAGICAL E-MAIL

"Good memory," Coach said approvingly. "For every person I've coached that actually did what I said, this one tool made the phone ring off the hook. Now what did I just say that e-mail should be used for?"

"To inform, confirm, or get people on the phone," Rick replied, looking at his notes.

"Good. Now to implement our plan for your B's, we will use what we call the Guaranteed Response E-mail or GRE. You're going to send a simple e-mail to all your B's which will cause them to give you a call. On that call you are going to ask them how they are doing and what's new in their lives. Then you will ask them the *Am I the Chosen One* script. Do you remember that?" Coach asked.

"Oh yeah," Rick replied. "If you had a friend or neighbor who was looking to sell a home, who would you recommend they call?"

"Good," said Coach. "After you have that conversation, which will only take a few minutes, you'll know if they are an A, C, or even a D."

"Really?" Rick was trying to figure out what was so magical about the e-mail.

"Really. Your goal by the next call is to have no more B's in your database. Your Potential Champions will either be

Champions who promise to refer you, Friends & Family because you choose to stay in touch with them; or they'll be deleted because they already have an established relationship with another professional in your industry."

"Okay," Rick said, wondering how to make all that happen before the next call.

"Don't worry. The biggest danger is that you'll go hoarse from talking on the phone so much," Coach chuckled. "I'll send you the text of the Guaranteed Response E-mail as soon as we're done with the call."

"I don't have all their e-mail addresses. What about getting the ones I can't find on Google?" Rick asked. It seemed weird to be asking a guy his father's age for advice like this.

"Well, besides all those social media sites, one great way is to do a monthly drawing through direct mail. Call it the '12 Months of Christmas' or the 'Thank You Campaign'. Make the prize something significant that your target group will like: an iPod, gift certificates, or a flat-screen TV. Have them e-mail their entries and you've got the e-mail address. It also gives you a chance to communicate with them when they enter. Just reply to their entries. "

"Great," Rick said, satisfied.

"We've talked about how to move a relationship from a 5 to a 1 using e-mail. Let's talk about moving them from a 5 to a 6 or more. Are you familiar with Google Alerts?" Coach asked.

"Way ahead of you there, Coach," Rick answered proudly. "Michelle showed me those at a lunch and I have over 50 alerts now—Michelle, that membership chair, my competition, Don Dasick, my company and even the variations of my name. I've had some great responses from the ones I forward."

"That's good that you implemented what Michelle taught you," Coach encouraged. "Now there are other good uses for e-mail," Coach continued. "It's a great way to introduce people who need to connect and refer someone in your

Community. You can also use it to confirm appointments or pass on other important information, which you're already doing."

"Just don't use it to sell?" Rick asked.

"Don't use it to sell, persuade, influence, or, as you learned, to try to close a deal. And like all other forms of communication, you need to have a plan."

BUILDING YOUR ONLINE COMMUNITY

"So that means time blocking and focus, right?"

"Absolutely," Coach confirmed. "Approach your online Community the same way you approach your offline Community. Start with a plan. Organize them in a way that allows you to check on the most valuable people in your Community first. If your clients and Ambassadors are on social media, check on them every day. Friends & Family members can be less often. Make it a point to take these online relationships and build them offline at your Networking Stack. And remember that everything is public. E-mail can be forwarded. Stuff on the web will never go away, even if you delete it. So keep it professional; no bragging about your wild weekend with the boys."

"Yeah, I've had some friends make that mistake," Rick laughed. "Clients don't want to trust their future to someone who's joking about getting hammered every weekend, huh?"

"You got it. No politics or religion either. Once you've organized your online community into lists, you'll want to Communicate your Solutions to your Community just like you do offline. Post your Success Stories on a blog, your status updates, or anywhere else they'll get read. Share your outgoing and incoming referral goals at least once a month."

"You mean I should post something like, 'I want to give 100 referrals and receive 50 referrals this year'?" Rick asked. For a moment he saw Don's billboard in his mind. *My posts will be like billboards in my online Community. And they're free . . .*

"Exactly," Coach answered. "And then ask 'Who can I refer to you, or who do you know that needs real estate services?' The rest of the month post things that are positive, funny or interesting. Don't be sarcastic, conceited, or negative. Just be yourself."

"The new me, right?" Rick laughed.

"You got that right," Coach laughed. "Now I want to emphasize that while electronic communication is important, it's not necessary to the success of your business."

"Really?" Rick asked, incredulously. "You think someone could get by today without using e-mail and all those networking sites that are popping up?"

"Absolutely," Coach said. "I got over four hundred referrals a year for the last 20 years I was in sales, Rick. I didn't start using e-mail until right before I retired, and even then I only checked it once a day. That was way back when it took twenty minutes to get online anyway. But these are different times, and of course I just told you how useful electronic communication can be. It's just that what you do online will only be as effective as what you do offline."

"I see that," Rick agreed. "I guess it's a problem if it distracts you from your offline activities or makes you think you're getting out there when you really just need to get out there in real life."

"Now you're talking. I'm starting to think you might be learning a thing or two." Coach chuckled.

"Yeah, maybe," Rick laughed.

YOUR ONLINE COMMUNITY

Coach continued, "So you grow your online community exactly the way you grow your offline community. You come with the spirit of helpfulness and encouragement. You have a plan to use it to increase your phone calls, to cross-sell, or confirm your one-on-one appointments."

"Cross-sell?" Rick asked.

"Yes, that's when two people sell each other rather than themselves. For instance, you would e-mail a positive message about Michelle to your buyer-client and Michelle would send a positive e-mail to the same client. The cross-selling is ten times more powerful than you telling your client how great you are. Remember to blind copy the person you are cross-selling in the e-mail. You can also do it with social media sites," Coach finished.

"Yeah, that makes a lot of sense," Rick said thoughtfully.

"And if possible, use video on your social networking sites. That keeps it more personal," Coach suggested. "I like what this guy Gary Vaynerchuk says in his book *CRUSH IT!*: 'Now, though, the Internet and social networks – and the instant access to online communities (and the millions of people who will eventually join them) they provide – have pumped up word of mouth like it was on steroids.'[18] Now it's easier and faster for anyone to spread the word about your services to more people than ever before. This is an exciting time for the Generosity Generation."

They continued to talk through the details of Rick's use of video and his overall online communication plan, and determined that he would send his Guaranteed Response E-mail to twenty B's at a time to prevent him from getting overwhelmed. They practiced what he would say, focusing on the *Are You the Chosen One* script and went through various follow-up scenarios. They discussed putting his referral goals and the phrase "I'm here to help" in his e-mail signature. Coach then assigned

18. Gary Vaynerchuk, *CRUSH IT! Why Now is the Time to Cash in on Your Passion* (New York: HarperCollins, 2009), 36 and to see a list of resources, please see www.ReferralLibrary.com.

The New Rules of Marketing and PR by David Meerman Scott, and two audio books: *Permission Marketing* by Seth Godin and *CRUSH IT!* by Vaynerchuk. Finally Coach was ready to wrap up.

"Before I let you go, you asked me about my wife last week," Coach said gently. "Am I getting a wedding invitation anytime soon?"

"Probably," Rick said evenly. "But not from me."

"Oh really?" Coach inquired. He sounded genuinely concerned.

"Yeah, turns out it wasn't meant to be," Rick sighed.

"Well, I'm sorry to hear that," Coach said sympathetically. "But listen, don't be discouraged. She's out there, somewhere, I promise."

"Thanks, Coach."

Rick hung up the phone. Part of him wished he had told Coach the whole story and asked him for advice. He sighed as he updated his task lists with his action items and saw the Guaranteed Response E-mail in his inbox.

```
Subject: Hey, <<First_Name>> have a few quick specific
questions for you...

Hey, «First_Name»!

Hope all is well.

Wanted to touch base. I have a couple of specific
questions for you. Could you please call me at your
earliest free moment at <<Your_Phone_Number>>? It's not
an emergency, but when you have a second, please give
me a call. I promise to only take a minute or two of
your time. Thank you in advance.

Talk to you soon!

<<Your_First_Name>>
```

P.S. If somebody else answers, please let them
know that I need to talk to you. Thank you. That's
<<Your_Phone_Number>>.

Then he saw another e-mail pop up that had just been sent.
He opened it and his jaw dropped:

Hey Rick!

How's it going? Sorry you haven't made it by an open
house yet. Anyway, let me know when you're free for
lunch. I'd like to chat when you have the time.

Don.

TRANSFORMATION

"Listen, that landscaper you referred to me has made our facility look like a billion dollars," Harold said enthusiastically into the phone. "You said he was the best and you weren't kidding!"

"I'm so glad," Rick said, smiling. He knew Jeremy wouldn't let him down. Harold's business park had been suffering from turnover like a lot of places, and he knew he needed the best look for the best price to stay competitive.

"Look, you know I only do commercial deals," Harold said in a more serious tone, "but I've got a few people who need a guy for residential transactions. I'm sending them your way, okay?"

"That would be great," said Rick. "I'm really looking forward to serving them. Also, listen, if you need a commercial agent to help fill some of your retail spots, please let me know.

I've got a great guy in mind. And I'm really glad Jeremy did a great job for you. I knew he would."

IT BOILS DOWN TO EDUCATION & COMMUNICATION

"So I'm expecting a progress report, young man," Coach said with mock severity. "Any B's left in the Community?"

"Well, yes," Rick said apologetically. "But I went from 56 to only 3. Added 27 new Champions too! The Guaranteed Response E-mail and *Are You the Chosen One* language worked just like you said it would!"

"Rick, that's fantastic," Coach congratulated him. "Really, I can't tell you how many guys don't make it to this session at all, let alone actually do what I say to do."

"Oh, well great then," Rick said, pleasantly surprised.

"So what would you say your biggest challenge is these days?" Coach inquired.

"Well, first, thank you for doing the morning session. My challenge is not something I would have thought possible a few months ago," Rick laughed. "But honestly, even though I'm time blocking everything, I just feel like there aren't enough hours in the day."

"Sounds like it's time to hire an assistant," Coach said thoughtfully.

"Really?" Rick asked.

"Well, can you afford it?"

"Sure, I guess. I just had my best month ever. To tell you the truth though, I hardly think about numbers anymore," Rick replied.

"That's how it is when you become a full-fledged member of the Generosity Generation," Coach approved. "Focus on the people. When you take care of the people, the numbers will take care of themselves."

"Yeah, that's really true. And it feels a lot better to focus on the people. Still, I'm worried I'd ruin an assistant. I've heard from so many people that they can be more trouble than they're worth. I mean you spend half your day writing out their list of things to do," Rick mused.

"Yeah, lots of people do exactly that," Coach agreed. "But before you hire one, create a time block for your assistant based on the things you need done. Keep your favorite tasks and the most dollar productive activities for yourself and give the rest to the assistant."

"Dollar-productive activities?"

"Yes, your work in Influential Zone work and with clients, offers and counter-offers, current contracts, and then your showings. Then you've got your listing appointments and prospecting. That's how you maximize your efficiency. These are the activities that make you the most money per hour. The rest can be somebody else's job. And what do you think is the best way to get a good assistant?"

"Through referral?" Rick guessed.

"Exactly right. Not only do we need to Communicate Our Solutions to Our Community, but we need to Communicate Our Needs to Our Community. Write down all the characteristics of the perfect assistant and let your Ambassadors and Champions know. Your first assistant will most likely come from your Community."

"That's a great idea," Rick said, writing it down.

A SOLUTION FOR EVERY SOLUTION

"Now the biggest thing we're going to cover today is your initial consultation that you offer your clients," Coach explained. "You'll need to create these for buyers, sellers, investors and any other category of clients that you deal with."

"Okay," said Rick, jotting notes. "I have a listing consultation I always give to sellers."

"Very good. Now you just need to make sure you have presentations prepared for all the solutions you offer," Coach explained. "You tell them to meet you at the office, and that you'll only take up a few minutes of their time. It might seem unnecessary but it will end up saving you and your client time in the long run."

"How so?" Rick asked.

"Imagine that you're out of town and staying at a friend's house. It's storming outside, you guys get in late, and when he unlocks his door; he discovers that the power is out."

"Okay," Rick said. Not sure where Coach was going with this but Rick had learned by now that the lesson was coming soon.

"Well, it's pitch black in there, and he walks across the living room and says, 'Come on in. Watch that vase on your left: I bought it in Greece. Hang on, I've got some candles in the kitchen.' How fast do you walk through that room to follow him?"

"Not too fast," Rick answered. "I don't want to knock over that vase or anything else."

"Exactly. You've never been there before and the room is dark. Now if the lights come back on, will you feel confident to go find your friend in the kitchen?"

"Sure."

"Your most important One-on-One Meetings could very well be these client consultations. Giving a client an initial One-on-One Meeting that walks him through every step is like throwing on the lights to the process of buying, selling or investing," Coach explained. "It shows your professionalism right off the bat, builds trust, and gives them the confidence to move through the entire process more quickly.

"Now, Rick, we're about at the end of the road," Coach said, a hint of emotion in his voice. "Your last assignment is one you don't have to turn in, because it's one you'll never finish."

"That doesn't sound good," Rick said, forcing a laugh. He felt a little sentimental too.

EACH ONE TEACH ONE

"Well, I think you'll end up enjoying it," Coach assured him. "I'm sure you realize by now that you're not done with the Generosity Generation just because you're done with the Seven Sessions of the Seven Levels. You're really just getting started. But the next step is for you to begin teaching others what you've learned. To whom much is given, much is required. We call it Each One, Teach One."

"That sounds great, but I really don't think I'm ready," Rick said hesitantly.

"Of course you are!" Coach laughed. "You're ready because you're actually doing it. I didn't say you had to teach all of it, though. Not yet anyway."

"That's a relief," Rick answered. He thought back to his initial meeting with Michelle at EVT Restaurant. *That's what she was doing with me. She was teaching me about The Seven Levels of Communication and the Generosity Generation.*

"Eventually, you'll be able to explain all of the things we've discussed to anyone. But let me ask you this: of everything we've talked about, what would you be most excited to teach someone right now?"

"It's hard to say," Rick admitted, reaching for his notes. "The Blessings Book and affirmations from session one were huge for me, and the second session's 1st & 10 calls were really a turning point for my business." He flipped through a few pages and continued, "The Magic Question has made life so much easier too, and I've already explained how it works to some of my referral partners. Actually, come to think of it, I explained the Triangle of Trust from session four and got into a referral conversation."

"How'd you do that?" Coach asked.

"Well, it was kind of an accident. I used myself and the gentleman I was meeting with as two corners of the triangle. When I mentioned that a Connector would be the third corner, he said, 'Oh, you mean like my cousin who runs the local BNI[19] chapter?' Before I knew it, he had agreed to introduce me!"

"Great job, Rick," Coach encouraged. "I'll have to file that away for later. What about sessions five and six?"

"Definitely planning out the phone calls for the whole year and the Guaranteed Response E-mail," Rick answered. "But then there's the Success Stories . . . I wrote that one success story we talked about way back in Session #2 and I've used it on a postcard, on my blog, by e-mail, and over the phone with clients. It's like a Swiss Army Knife: one tool with a thousand uses."

"Good one, Rick," Coach laughed. "See, you've already come up with your own metaphor!"

"Yeah, I guess so," Rick laughed. "It's interesting. I knew to write notes, but now I have a strategy for it. I knew to make phone calls, but now I have a strategy for it. I knew to network, but now I have a strategy that works. And I guess if I had to name one more, I'd say the Generosity Generation. I think a lot of people realize in the back of their heads that there's something different about doing business in today's world, but they've never thought it through so they're still using the same old tactics and in some cases using new tools the wrong way, you know?"

19. Business Network International (www.BNI.com) is a networking organization founded by Dr. Ivan Misner

"I agree, Rick, I agree. And I think that's very insightful. I think you've become a lot more thoughtful."

"Now that we're talking about it, you're right. I've grown a lot. The least I can do is to continue to share what I've learned with others."

"And that's what will take your own learning to the next level," Coach continued. "If you keep teaching, you'll be hungrier to learn more. Taking responsibility for explaining it to someone else will give you ownership of the material. You'll have a new benefit – you provide value to others through the teachings of Seven Levels. When you ask people what their biggest challenges are, you'll have an arsenal of answers to help them." Rick thought about the lunch with Michelle again, and then quickly turned his focus back to the call.

"Yeah, it's like what you were saying about affirming others and trying to help them accomplish their goals. Now I can help a lot of people and know that as I do, they'll help me too."

"Exactly," Coach agreed. "I had my doubts about you at the beginning, Rick. I was hopeful, but unsure. I want you to know I'm proud of what you've accomplished. And I'm excited to hear more about what you're doing in the future. Before I let you go, I'd like to ask you a couple of questions."

"Sure," Rick replied.

"First, something I have found in my coaching is that those who persevere, the really special ones, such as yourself, tend to know other special professionals. So with that in mind, out of all the people you know, who is a real estate agent, mortgage professional, or other entrepreneur who is a candidate to invest in themselves by getting coached?"

"Well," Rick replied, "this applies to so many of my networking connections, referral partners, and colleagues. Do you work with attorneys?"

"Sure do. Anybody in sales or marketing who wants to grow their business by word of mouth," Coach answered.

Rick had a couple of names in mind and immediately gave them to Coach. Coach got the information and Rick promised to call them before 4:00 P.M.

"Secondly, I'd like to ask you to stay in touch," Coach said. Rick noted the respect in his voice.

"So this isn't goodbye forever?" Rick laughed.

"No," Coach answered warmly. "No more two-hour calls, probably. But I'm always around, and Jay lets me know what's going on. We'll definitely be in touch."[20]

THE CONFESSION

They said their goodbyes and Rick took a moment to reflect on how much his life had changed. He left messages for the two people he had recommended to Coach and jotted a quick POWER Note. Then he looked at his watch and realized there were just twenty minutes before his appointment with Don. He quickly grabbed his briefcase and headed out to EVT Restaurant. *Coach was right about the benefits of never getting lost,* he thought as he pulled into the parking lot, greeted Katherine, and got seated by Jo Ellen at his usual booth. He knew it wasn't Michelle's day to come in, but he looked up, half hoping he would see her anyway.

"Hey, Buddy," Don said with his customary smoothness as he sat down across the table. He turned to Jo Ellen who had just come to take their drink orders. "J&B straight up, honey."

"Sure," Jo Ellen replied, skillfully hiding her surprise. "Iced tea for you, Rick?"

---

20. If you are interesting in being coached by a Certified Referral Coach, please see www. CertifiedReferralCoaching.com. If you are interested in becoming a Certified Referral Coach, please see www.CertifiedReferralCoach.com.

"Yes, thanks Jo Ellen," Rick replied, smiling. She left to get their drinks.

"First time here?" Don asked sarcastically.

"Hey, I'm a sucker for hearing my name. They treat me good and I keep coming back," Rick answered nonchalantly. The two continued with small talk about Don's latest triumphs while Jo Ellen returned with their drinks and took their lunch orders.

"So I gotta ask you, buddy," Don said, shifting in his seat as he downed the last of his scotch, "did you sell your soul to the devil or what?"

"I'm sorry?" Rick asked, genuinely confused.

"Your numbers," Don replied, signaling to Jo Ellen that he was ready for another. "Let's be real. You and I had nearly identical numbers two months ago, and I thought that was a miracle. But a miracle as in, one time only . . . a fluke . . . you know, temporary suspension of the laws of physics . . ."

"Sure," Rick chuckled. *What is he talking about?*

"But then," Don said, sipping his second drink, "then you went and beat me the last two months straight . . . bad. Your numbers are insane and you're making it look easy. So that's why I'm asking . . . what's your secret?"

"No secret," Rick said calmly. "Just the Seven Levels stuff I learned at that seminar and in my coaching sessions. Real simple stuff, but powerful."

"You're kidding!" Don said, a little too loud. He looked around, leaned forward, and lowered his voice as Jo Ellen set their salads down and quietly refilled Rick's iced tea. "Are you really telling me you're doing that many transactions because some guy in a turtleneck told you that nice guys finish first?"

"Well there's a little more to it than that, but basically, yes," Rick answered, taking a bite of his salad.

"Well then maybe I need to sign up to drink the Kool-Aid too," Don laughed, cutting a piece of bread and buttering it.

"What do you mean?" Rick asked. "You're doing great. I know you moved three of those units downtown..."

"Yeah, well, I can't seem to move 'em fast enough, you know?" Don looked into his glass.

Why are we having this meeting? Rick thought. *Is Don Dasick really asking me for help?* They continued talking shop while Jo Ellen brought their entrees.

"What did you mean about not moving properties fast enough?" Rick asked quietly as he took a bite of his crab cake. Rick realized how naturally the question came out. *He's going to bite my head off...*

"Oh, nothing," Don said casually. "This is damn good steak, Rick."

"Yeah, they know how to do it here. Happy cows or something," Rick chuckled.

Don drained his glass and looked Rick right in the eyes. "You've seen my billboard right? The one right off the highway?"

"Sure," Rick said, suppressing the urge to roll his eyes. "Everyone has."

"Well, son, do you know what those billboards cost?"

"No, not really," Rick said. He realized how long it had been since he had even thought about advertising.

"More than most people make in a year, Rick. Sure, I can do deals for the hot shots, but they all expect special treatment. My sales went down when everyone else's did, but my expenses didn't. I won't drag you through the details, but the truth is..." Don paused as if trying to decide how much more he wanted to say. Rick said nothing. He had never in his life imagined that the great Don Dasick could sound this vulnerable, slouched in a chair across the table from him. Rick poked his crab cake and examined it as if he was trying to catalogue each ingredient for a restaurant review.

"The truth is," Don continued in a voice just above a whisper, "I'm meeting with my accountant this month to decide whether I need to file for bankruptcy. I saw your numbers and I thought you must have some secret. Pretty funny, huh? Dial Don is Deep in Debt Don!" he laughed bitterly and cut another piece of his steak. Both men winced as the knife squeaked loudly against the plate.

"Of course not," Rick said, his voice filled with sympathy. "Don, you don't have to declare bankruptcy. Just get rid of the billboards and the bus ads. You're still moving plenty of properties; you'd be above water in no time!"

"Are you crazy?" Don asked, again a little too loud. "That's like announcing I'm broke to the world. Then I really will be out of business."

"No, listen to me," Rick urged. "You saw my numbers. Would you believe me if I told you that I haven't spent a penny on personal advertising in over three months? And I'll never do personal promotion again. "

"What?" Don was speechless.

"It's true. You haven't seen my face on anything, have you? That's what the Generosity Generation is all about. It's referrals. It's relationships. It's about focusing on people and letting the numbers take care of themselves."

Don stared at him across the table as if he was speaking a foreign language.

"Listen," Rick continued, "You know that condo I sold downtown? I sold that for a woman, Terri, that had just finished her doctorate and is moving away. She was referred to me by her cousin David and his wife Deanna, a couple that I just helped buy their first home. So what do you think I did when I helped Terri sell her condo?"

"I have no idea," Don said, forcing a bemused smile as he buttered another piece of bread.

"I called David and Deanna and let them know that Terri's condo sold and how happy she is. As Deanna and I were talking, she remembers that one of the women at her gym is looking for a larger house. So she's e-mailing me next week to introduce me. Not only that, but David and Deanna were referred to me by my friend Josh. I'll call him tomorrow morning and update him on both sales. Jay calls it The Great Re-Trace. It reinforces to them that they did the right thing by referring me. I've only been doing this a few months, and it's already building on itself."

"You know what I found out the other day?" Don asked, shaking his head.

"What's that?"

"Those Hollywood folks I sold to—they knew my ex-wife. She taught piano to their kids. That's why they called me," Don admitted.

"So you see?" Rick encouraged. "It's real, Don. You could do it too, I know you could."

"Do you know how old I am, Rick? I sold my first million when you were going to your junior prom. Now my wife is leaving, my kids hate me, and my only friends are the bloodsucking ad reps who want a piece of the action."

There was a long silence while the two men continued to eat. Rick looked at Don across the table and remembered how he had felt before Seven Levels. Don's hair was still jet black, colored for sure, but there were wrinkles sneaking up around the eyes. Although his suit was of the highest quality, Rick noticed just the slightest bit of wear around his shirt collar. He tried to think of what Coach would say in this kind of situation. "What do *you* think you should do?" Rick finally asked.

Don thought for a minute. "I think I need to fly out to see my kids," he finally said. "They live with my first wife in Southern California. The boy's getting ready to graduate from high school . . ."

"That's great," Rick offered enthusiastically.

"Yeah, everyone says they grow up fast, but it's even worse when they live so far away. I don't know if they would even recognize me," Don said sadly, looking down at the remainder of his meal. "Their mom, she was with me when all we could afford was a little one bedroom apartment, you know? I was an idiot to leave her for Mindy . . . but anyway, you were telling me about your little secret society," he finished with a laugh.

"Yeah," Rick smiled. "I'm telling you, Don, you're not too old. I saw a woman at least ten years older than you that was working the Seven Levels and getting it done. She was about this tall, too." Rick held his hand slightly above the height of the table.

Don laughed, "You're kidding me!"

"No, I'm serious," Rick said, laughing too. "Listen, Jay's going to be back in town this weekend doing another seminar. I know I can get you a ticket. Why don't you just come and check it out for yourself?"

"I think I'm a lost cause, brother," Don laughed, polishing off the last bite of steak.

"Well, no harm in having a look, right? What do you have to lose?" Rick offered.

"You know what?" Don said, looking up from his plate. "I might just do it." Jo Ellen cleared their dishes and brought some coffee while the two wrapped up the conversation. Rick learned that Don's first wife was still working as a piano teacher and that his daughter was in her second year of college. He wondered what it was like for Don to be so far away from them. Rick felt his phone vibrate as the calendar alerted him that his next appointment was in 15 minutes. Both men looked at their watches and Don rose to shake hands and say goodbye.

"You hanging around, buddy?" Don asked as he grabbed his briefcase.

"Yeah, I've got a 1:00 here in a few. Listen, I'm going to send you an e-mail to remind you about this weekend, okay?"

"You betcha," Don smiled and turned to leave.

Did that just happen? Rick shook his head. He sipped his coffee and then checked his phone. He started an e-mail to Don but stopped and opened his calendar instead. He created a new appointment for 4:00 P.M. He thumbed, "Dial Don."

He also had several texts which he scrolled through, responding to each one methodically. Then he came to one and paused. He reread it twice. He checked the time it was sent and the number from which it came. He wanted more than anything to cancel his appointment due to start five minutes from now, but he knew he couldn't.

Quickly, he texted back: *Karen, thx 4 the message! In mtg until 4. Will call you then. Keep Fri night open pls. I know you're hdng out of twn, but it's important. IOU1. Thx. See you Fri! Rick.*

JAY MICHAELS
SPEAKS AGAIN

10

For whoever exalts himself will be humbled, and whoever humbles himself will be exalted.

MATTHEW 23:12 (NIV)

RICK'S EYES opened two minutes before his alarm was due to go off. He stretched, rolled over, and took a drink of water. He opened his Blessings Book to write his Appreciations and Affirmations.

I APPRECIATE MY HEALTH.

I APPRECIATE MY FAMILY AND THEIR CONTINUED SUPPORT.

I APPRECIATE MY FRIENDS FOR BEING THERE FOR ME.

I APPRECIATE THE OPPORTUNITY TO DO MEANINGFUL WORK THAT WILL HELP OTHERS.

I APPRECIATE HAVING PLENTY AND BEING ABLE TO GIVE EXCESS TO OTHERS.

He then jotted his affirmations. Finished with his Blessings Book, Rick sprang out of bed and went to brush his teeth, repeating his affirmations by heart as he looked in the mirror. In three minutes, he was in his workout gear and headed out for a five-mile run. Checking his watch on the way back up the stairs he realized he had beaten his best time for that route. His thoughts drifted to the half-marathon coming up in a couple of months.

He took a quick shower and began to dress. He flexed in the mirror. *Was that an ab muscle?* His clothes were waiting for him—slacks, sport coat, shirt and tie, even his socks . . . *I never thought I'd be the kind of guy that would lay out his socks for the week.* He tied his tie and thought about the people he was going to call today. He could see their faces and their kids' faces and picture the kind of houses they would like. He thought about the many hours they would spend and memories they would share in their new homes and how gratifying it was to be part of making that happen. He carefully reviewed two contracts he had drawn up last night and placed them in his briefcase which was in its accustomed spot by his desk.

Rick finished listening to his audio book on the way to the office and greeted Lisa with a warm smile. "Good morning!"

"Good morning, Rick," she smiled back. "Michelle called. I'm sure she left a message."

"Great!" Rick said, trying to temper his reaction. "Thanks for telling me. How did Mary do at States?"

"Third in long jump, fourth in the 4x400 relay," Lisa answered proudly.

"Well, tell her congratulations for me, okay?"

"I sure will. Oh, and thanks so much for helping out my cousin!" Lisa added. "She's so excited about the condo."

"I'm glad," Rick answered warmly. "I knew it would be perfect for her." Rick entered his office and put on his headset for his 1st & 10. Everything inside him wanted to call Michelle right then, but he knew the 1st & 10 had to be done now. *Do it Now!* Rick tapped the band on his wrist. Another hour wouldn't make a difference. He reviewed his list, checked the first number, and dialed.

Forty-five minutes later he had a referral and six action items. He got to work on his new list and looked at his watch. It would be okay to call Michelle now. She would probably be done with her 1st & 10 too.

"Hi, Rick!" she said warmly. The elation of her engagement must have worn off a bit, but she was still the same kind, friendly person.

"Hi, Michelle," Rick answered. "Thanks for returning my call. How've you been?"

"Well, busy of course," Michelle laughed. "But good. Just trying to coordinate wedding plans along with all the business stuff, you know?"

"Sure," Rick said sympathetically. "If anyone can manage, you can. Listen, you're going tonight, right?"

"Of course," Michelle answered. "You'll be in the front, right?"

"Yeah, Coach hooked me up," Rick laughed. "Is Alan going to make it?"

"Not this time," Michelle said. "He had to go to San Diego to take a deposition."

"Gotcha," Rick said, feeling his cheeks flush a bit. "Well, I just wanted to let you know that I'm bringing a few people I want you to meet."

"Great," Michelle responded. "You know I love meeting new people."

"Most of them will be great business contacts, one is Don— the guy from the billboards," Rick continued.

"Don Dasick is coming?" Michelle asked. "Wow, really? That's . . . interesting. How'd you talk him into that?"

"Well, he came to me. Long story that I'll definitely plan to tell you sometime, but there's someone I'm going to introduce you to that wants to talk to you about more personal stuff. I really can't say more than that, but I wanted to give you a heads up."

"Okay," Michelle said. "That's fine. I'd love to meet whoever it is, I'm sure."

"Thanks, Michelle. I'm really looking forward to tonight."

"Me, too!" They said their goodbyes, and Rick quickly updated his database with a few more notes. He had no idea how tonight was going to go, but he was grateful he had a busy day ahead to distract him until it got there.

THE TESTIMONIAL

The auditorium once again buzzed with smiles, hugs, and happy greetings as more and more people seemed to pour in through the doors. Rick fidgeted in his seat. He turned and smiled as Michelle, who had been talking to one of the people she invited took the seat five down from him. He leaned over to shake Don's hand as he arrived just before the light dimmed and the screens dropped. Don shrugged his shoulders as if to say "Here goes nothing!" The look on his face reminded Rick of how he had felt at the last conference.

He reflected on how different this experience was. Last time, he had felt like such a fish out of water, and now he felt at home. He knew what to expect, but he was still excited. He glanced around the room. It was a different auditorium and Rick estimated there were at least twice as many in attendance. *Word gets around*, he smiled to himself. The Generosity Generation was growing.

After the introductory video, Jay entered to twice the applause that had greeted him a few months earlier. *Wow, it's loud in here!* Rick rose and clapped with the rest. He glanced over his shoulder. *Where is she?* He nervously checked his cell phone, now on vibrate but not turned off. No message.

Jay greeted the crowd warmly and launched into the affirmations. Rick participated with enthusiasm and then pulled out his notepad as Jay began the first part of his presentation. Rick marveled at how easily he was able to follow his talk this time. Of course there were new insights and new information, but he already knew how it connected together. He glanced sideways at Don to see how he was reacting. Don was shifting in his seat, but paying attention. *I think there's hope for the old guy yet.* Minutes seemed to fly by as Rick filled his pages with notes.

"And that's why everyone who is doing this is not just adding to their business: they're seeing exponential increase," Jay explained as the crowd cheered. "Now before we take our break, I want you guys to hear from one of our newest coaching graduates. He's been applying these principles for just a few months and he's already broken all his personal records and even some records at his brokerage. Join me in welcoming Rick Masters!"

Rick took a deep breath and rose to join Jay on stage. He saw Don raise his eyebrows in surprise as he passed him. Rick turned his head in time to throw Michelle a quick wink as she smiled supportively.

"Thank you, Jay. Great to be here tonight," Rick said taking the microphone confidently.

"Hi, Rick. Now you just graduated from our coaching program. Why don't you tell us about how your business was going when you started out?"

"Sure," Rick responded. He tried not to think about how many people were listening, but instead focused on the remarks he had prepared. "To tell you the truth, I was about to look for another job. I never thought I'd consider going back to accounting, but I was almost there. I hadn't had a sale in several months, and I had properties sitting on the market so long they were becoming protected historical sites!" The crowd chuckled appreciatively.

"So what turned it around, Rick?" Jay asked.

"To be honest, it was me that got turned around first. My business was doing terrible, but so was I. I was overweight, depressed and cynical. I had lost the will to try. Coaching gave me more than a new outlook on my business. It gave me a new outlook on life."

"Wow, that's powerful," said Jay. "So how are things going now?"

"Well, I can't even begin to describe it. I've done more transactions in the last six weeks than I did in the previous two years. I've averaged four referrals a week since I got my database in order and started with my 1st & 10 calls. I'm time blocking my schedule so I always know what's supposed to be happening. Obviously, this has been great for my personal finances, but the crazy thing is, I don't even care about that much anymore. Six months ago, I was obsessed with money. Now, I'm obsessed with helping people. It's a much better feeling, let me tell you." Rick glanced down at the front row and saw Michelle beaming up at him. He saw Don looking down at his lap.

"That's great, Rick. What's your favorite story about helping someone?" Jay asked.

"There are so many that it's hard to pick, but I would say helping a woman named Sandra close on her first home five weeks ago. She called me because her sister works in my dentist's office. I had to get a filling three months ago and before using the Ultimate Memory Jogger, I hadn't even thought to make sure that my dentist, doctor, and so many others were in my database. Anyway, Sandra is a single mother of two. She's been working and going to school at night, getting her nursing degree. I sat down with her and found out immediately what was most important to her: school districts, safe neighborhoods and resale value. I made sure that every house we looked at fit those specifications and I can't tell you how many people she works with at the hospital who have called me since."

"That's great, Rick," Jay said proudly.

"But that's not even the best part. Of course it felt wonderful to see her settle into that house with the backyard for her kids to play in and know that they're going to one of the best elementary schools in the state. But I told Sandra's success story on a postcard and in an e-mail to my Community. I shared it on my blog. At this point, Sandra's story has generated at least 12 referrals. It's really true, Jay. Success attracts success."

"Rick, that's wonderful. Serving people is what the Generosity Generation is all about. Is there anything else you want to say to the folks here before we take this break?"

"I'd just like to add that when I sat here a few months ago, I was just like some of you: I had no idea what was going on. I heard some good ideas, some stuff I didn't understand, and some amazing testimonials that seemed too good to be true. I was on the fence about coaching: it was a lot of money and I was getting behind on almost all my bills. I went for it because I didn't know what else to do. I didn't want to leave the business, and I knew if I didn't do something, I would have to. I'm here to tell you it was the best decision I ever made."

THE BREAK

Rick placed the microphone back on the stand and returned to his seat to applause. He saw Michelle radiant with pride and caught his breath as he saw Karen in the seat next to his. At last! He had been worried she wouldn't show up.

"Nice job!" she leaned over and whispered in his ear. "You're really into this stuff, huh?"

"Yeah," he replied. The lights were on now and people were moving around for the break. "Thanks for coming Karen. You can let me know if it works for lawyers!"

"Yeah, I'll check it out. Listen, I've got to get home and prepare for a jury trial next week," Karen said apologetically.

"Of course," Rick said quickly. He glanced over to check on Don, who was shaking hands with an Ambassador and chatting it up. "Come with me." He led her over to Michelle, who was speaking to a younger woman. They waited for her to finish and then Rick introduced her to Karen.

"Karen is an old friend of mine, Michelle. She also knows Alan," Rick said tentatively.

"Of course," Michelle said, offering Karen her hand and smiling. "I think Alan mentioned you to me."

"Hi, Michelle," Karen said kindly. "Listen, I want to congratulate you on your engagement, but I wonder if we could chat in private for a minute."

"Sure," Michelle said, a little taken aback. "We can step outside, if you don't mind the cold."

"That's great," Karen answered. "Rick, I'm going to have to take off after this, but this was cool. I might want to come back some other time, actually."

"That would be wonderful, Karen. Thanks," Rick shook her hand and waved to Michelle. *Here goes nothing,* he thought to himself as he saw the two women heading for an exit sign. The room was still abuzz.

"Mr. Masters?" a voice said behind him.

"Call me Rick, please," he said instinctively as he turned to shake the hand of a twenty-something young man in twill pants and a sweater.

"Hi, I just wanted to say that I really enjoyed what you shared. I've had my license for two months now, and I'd love to know more about what you're doing in your business. Depending on what area of town you specialize in, I may also have a referral for you."

"Sure," Rick said agreeably. "What do you want to know?" He saw over the young man's shoulder that a small line was forming. *All these people want to talk to me?* He answered the young man's questions, they exchanged cards and Rick shook hands with the next person in line, a woman about his age. He repeated the process with everyone he could get to before the lights flashed, indicating that they needed to take their seats again.

As he returned to his seat, he turned his head anxiously to see if Michelle was sitting down yet. She wasn't there. Jay returned to the stage to another standing ovation and she was still nowhere to be found. Rick looked at his watch. He reached for his notepad and tried to look around the room without being obvious. Still no Michelle.

Rick looked at his phone. No message. Well, he had done all he could do; the rest was out of his hands. He took out his pen and focused his attention on the stage.

ANOTHER LUNCH
OF A LIFETIME

11

"What lies behind us and what lies before us are tiny matters compared to what lies within us."

RALPH WALDO EMERSON

"I THINK IT'S FINALLY starting to sink in," Michelle said softly as she sipped her tea. Theresa placed some bread on the table and slipped away silently.

"I'm so sorry," Rick said, reaching across the table to give her hand a quick squeeze.

"That's just the thing," Michelle said looking at him, "I thought I would be sorry too. But I don't think I am."

"Really?" Rick asked, trying not to sound too excited.

"Really. I mean, I'm a little angry," she laughed. "When Karen told me that Alan had asked her to go away for the weekend, 'just like old times,' I was in shock. I mean I couldn't even get mad, because I couldn't process what she was saying."

"I can't tell you how much I agonized over what to do," Rick interjected. "When Karen texted me and told me what Alan had done, I kept asking her if she was sure she didn't misunderstand him . . . I couldn't believe it either . . ."

"Rick," Michelle smiled warmly. "You did the right thing. I mean, how could I marry someone like that? Of course I needed to know, even if it was painful. I'm just blessed that you and Karen kept in touch and that she let you know what was going on. I mean, what are the odds of that?"

"Well, about that . . ." Rick said hesitantly.

"Yes?" Michelle asked, raising her eyebrows.

"Well, it might not have been as coincidental as you think. Karen and I dated a long time ago. It ended fine, but I hadn't spoken to her in years. When you told me that Alan had dated Karen, I actually looked her up."

"Oh," Michelle said, taking another sip of her tea.

"Honestly, I wanted to know what she thought of him. I had no idea he would contact her again, of course. But I didn't trust Alan from the first day we met, and when you said you guys were getting married . . . I promise I didn't think I would uncover anything like this."

"Rick," Michelle said gently, "it doesn't matter. It all worked out for the best, and now I guess I can just say that I'm blessed to have a friend that cared about me enough to ask the questions I should have been asking all along." Rick breathed a sigh of relief. "The truth is, after the conference, I realized that I was never really in love with Alan. I was in love with what I thought Alan represented."

"What do you mean?" Rick asked.

"Well, he's a successful lawyer. He's nice looking and ambitious. He's the right age. I never thought a guy like that would come along, let alone be interested in me. I guess I'm still more superficial than I thought."

"No," Rick said quickly. "No, you're not superficial. You just see the good in everyone. I'm sure Alan has some potential in there somewhere, and you just honed in on that. And honestly,

Michelle, any guy would be lucky to have you." He squeezed her hand again.

"Thank you," she smiled. Rick thought he detected a little flush in her cheeks. Or was that her makeup? Did she even wear makeup? If she did it looked really natural.

"Listen," Rick continued. "I know you just got out of a relationship. So there's a lot I'd like to say that I'm going to save for another time. I would just love it if . . . if . . . "

"Yes?" Michelle asked, smiling.

"If I could be your standing lunch date on Tuesdays for a while. How does that sound?"

"It sounds great," Michelle laughed. "It sounds like the best way I can think of to start my Networking Stack."

Theresa refilled their drinks and Rick thought he noticed a smile on her face. Rick and Michelle passed the next half hour catching up on each other's lives and making plans for the second Lunch and Learn at Rick's firm. One o'clock came quickly.

"Well, I see Don in the parking lot," Rick said, almost reluctantly.

"And Karen just texted me that she's on her way," Michelle said. "What an unusual way to become friends!"

"She's got the potential to be a rainmaker. She can learn a lot from you," Rick smiled.

"Well, I can't believe Don Dasick signed up for coaching!" Michelle laughed.

"Yeah, we'll know it for sure when the billboard comes down!" Rick rose to meet Don in the foyer and take his place at his regular booth. He and Michelle exchanged a brief hug. He held on for an extra second. "Call me anytime, okay?" he whispered in her ear. *She smells nice.*

"I will," she whispered back. The two parted and sat down with their respective 1:00 appointments.

"Rick, you won't believe who I have for coaching!" Don said, sitting down in the booth and ordering a coffee. "The guy's older than I am! He's like a drill sergeant!"

"Really?" Rick asked, suppressing a chuckle. "Tell me about him."

Theresa brought drinks to everyone.

"Michelle, you look amazing. I never would have believed you'd just been through . . ." Karen paused, not sure of how to end the sentence.

"Thanks," Michelle said, her trademark smile flashing. "I feel great. I can't thank you enough for being honest with me. That's one of the qualities I value most, and if you don't mind me saying it's refreshing to find in a lawyer." The two women laughed and began to share about their lives as if they had grown up next door to one another.

"Coffee, black," Don ordered. "I still can't drink iced tea. I'm cutting back on the scotch, but I've got my limits."

"No worries," Rick laughed. "We've all got to start somewhere."

EPILOGUE: THE GENEROSITY GENERATION

12

"When you give someone a book, you don't give him just paper, ink, and glue. You give him the possibility of a whole new life."

CHRISTOPHER MORLEY

RICK GATHERED SEVERAL PAPERS off his desk and stacked them neatly before putting them in a file folder. The room was full of boxes. It was hard to believe he was going to say good-bye to his condo after twelve years.

"What should I do with these?" Michelle called to him from across the room. She was holding an armful of cards and letters.

"Gosh, I don't know," Rick said, looking at them. "I can't throw them away . . ."

"I know what you mean," Michelle agreed. "Why don't we put them in a box for now and decide later."

"Good idea," Rick walked over and took them from her, and went to retrieve a shoe box from his closet. As much as it was easier to sort through all his stuff with Michelle's help, he was relieved that he had gotten rid of most of his useless junk during his coaching sessions.

He returned to his office with the box and started to place the pile of correspondence inside. He paused over a few:

> RICK,
>
> JUST WANTED TO DROP YOU A NOTE TO THANK YOU FOR YOUR PRESENTATION TODAY. YOUR IDEA ON CALLING 10 PEOPLE AS SOON AS I GET TO THE OFFICE SOUNDS GREAT. I'LL LET YOU KNOW HOW IT GOES!
>
> SMITTY

Rick smiled as he reopened the next one, which had just come a few days ago.

> Rick,
>
> Can't thank you enough for dragging me to the conference. This was my first month in the black in what feels like forever. Coach is kicking my you-know-what, so I don't even need to tell you how that's going. You know what's funny? Don't even miss seeing my face all over town, and I'm sure you don't either!
>
> Don
>
> P.S. You'll love this: Dial Don is now Dialing Don! Give me a call and let's grab lunch, my treat.

Rick heard the doorbell ring. It was a package which he signed for.

"What is it?" called Michelle from the living room, where she sat packing up the few pictures and decorations that Rick had accumulated in his years of bachelor living.

"I don't know," he answered, joining her on the floor. He put his arm around her shoulders and offered it to her. "Why don't you open it?" She took it from him and pulled the tab to open the top of the large padded envelope. She pulled out a brand new volume and both of their eyes opened wide with disbelief.

"This isn't supposed to be out for weeks!" Michelle said with excitement. "Oh, and there's a note, too." They opened it and read the familiar handwriting together,

> Rick,
>
> This won't be on the bookshelves for another three weeks, but got two signed copies ahead of time. I'm giving my second copy to you, trusting that you'll share it with Michelle. I expect to be getting that invitation in the mail real soon.
>
> Coach
>
> P.S. Rick, you'll notice that we've forgotten one very important strategy in here. You know it, but to get it or to share it, please go to the web site.[21]

"But we haven't told anyone," Rick said, rereading the words and pulling Michelle close to him.

"Yeah, Coach just knows," Michelle laughed. "He probably knew before either of us."

"You're right," Rick agreed. "Besides, everyone will know soon enough."

---

21. To see the special Forgotten Strategy just for readers who've completed (7L) to this point, go to www.ForgottenStrategy.com.

GLOSSARY OF TERMS

Asterisks (*) indicate in-text definition.

1st & 10: First thing upon arriving at the office, make ten phone calls. These should be written or printed the night before with name, phone number, and the reason for your call (and perhaps opportunities presented by other person). (Pages 62,* 90, 113, 129, 141, 144)

Affirmation: Positive self-talk. Phrases and sentences that begin with "I am...". State what you want to achieve in the future using the present tense. Want to be a best-selling author? Your affirmation would be: "I am a best-selling author." (Pages 21,* 22, 23, 50–51, 58, 129, 140, 143)

Ambassadors ("A+" Level Contact): Those who have referred you more than once in the last 12 months. (Pages 15,* 21, 34, 64, 91, 105–107, 119, 124)

Ambassador Development System (formerly New Contact System): A system for rapidly establishing connections with a new contact. Once a business card is received that person goes into the Ambassador Development System which would include connecting via all social media (Facebook, Twitter, LinkedIn, etc.), including information in database, perhaps sending out a VIP form if not already completed, and adding to any follow-up programs.

Appreciations: Statements of appreciation. Phrases and sentences that begin with "I appreciate...". What you appreciate, appreciates. If you want more of something in your life, appreciate what you have of something in your life now. If you want more great relationships in your life ... appreciate the ones you have. (Page 139*)

"Are You the Chosen One" Script: Script to determine whether you would be recommended when a need for your services arose. "If you had a friend or neighbor who was looking to sell their home, who would you recommend they call first?" (Pages 98–99,* 117, 121, 126)

Blessings Book: A journal to write your five Appreciations and your five Affirmations. Many professionals use this as their note-taking "Inbox" throughout the day as well. See www.ReferralLibrary.com for more. (Pages 49,* 62, 129, 139–140)

Board of Advisors: Group of contacts brought in to advise a business owner on an event or topic. (Page 107)

Champions ("A" Level Contact): Those who have referred you one person in the last 12 months. (Pages 105,* 106–108, 117–119)

Communication Plans: When, how, and how often you will be contacting the members of your Community. (Pages 101*–123)

Communication Pyramid: The illustration to show The Seven Levels of Communication. (Figures 2-1 through 2-4, page 37*)

Community: The people you know and have information on. Database, network, and community are similar in meaning, but a community connotes communication. (Page 26*)

Connector: Person with a lot of contacts and a willingness to grow their network and help others grow their network. (Page 65*–67, 74, 79, 94, 130)

The 7 Steps to Connecting with Connectors

1. Helpful Spirit—Go with the idea of helping whoever you meet.
2. Call. Call the Organizer or Membership Chair (person in charge) to ask them a) how are introductions done—formal or informal? and b) who the top 3 or 4 most influential networkers are at the meeting.
3. Google. Before the event, Google the three or four people the organizer mentioned and the organizer.
4. Punctual. Arrive 30 minutes early for the event wearing your name badge on the right side of your outfit.
5. Introductions. Have the Organizer introduce you to the Connectors.
6. FROG. Use FROG to build rapport. Family, Recreation, Occupation, and Goals.
7. Follow-up and Follow-through. Get them scheduled for One-on-One Meetings and send a POWER Note.

Cross-Selling: A subset of the Triangle of Trust where one professional speaks highly about another professional to a client or consumer. The favor is returned by the other professional. (Page 121*)

Customer Relationship Management (CRM): database of contacts. Tool for keeping track of your Community.

Demographic Farm: a group of people tied by something other than geography. Gender, hobbies, interests, job, people, entertainment, etc. are a few of the ways a demographic group can be separated. (Page 108*)

Delete or Drip ("D" Level Contact): Those who don't belong in your Community. Delete their information from your database to focus on more valuable, energizing, and pleasant relationships. (Page 105*)

DiSCOVERING: Vision exercise in which one chooses four people with differing DiSC behavioral styles and writes about how they are consistent with that behavioral style while also showing some characteristics of the other styles.

The DiSCovery: Poem by Michael J. Maher. Smile like Everyone's an I, Care like Everyone's an S, Prepare like Everyone's a C, and Sell like Everyone's a D. This poem is a reminder of how to build trust. (Page 77*)

Drip or Drip Campaign: A follow-up system typically consisting of e-mails. Drip is for those who don't belong in your BOOST!150 but you still want to continue communication.

The Ego Era: A period of time where personal promotion, self-absorption, and image advertising were rampant. It was all about the business owner, real estate agent, or mortgage professional. It was about the I. "All about me" was the slogan of this era and "AllAboutMe.com" Web sites were the norm. These businesses fed the ego. (Pages 2, 42)

Epitaph: Short text inscribed on a tombstone—"life's slogan." (Page 23*)

F-Bomb: A series of POWER Notes, electronic communication, informational items, phone calls, and perhaps One-on-One Meetings. The f-word in business is Follow-up. You should have a system of follow-up for your new networking contacts. (Pages 79–80*)

Family & Friends ("C" Level Contact): Casual level of contact. (Pages 106,* 108, 119)

Feel-felt-found script: Used to alleviate fears and overcome objections. Also shows credibility and experience. Example: "I understand how you feel, Mr. Client. I've had many clients who have felt the same way and what they found is that by doing this they were more comfortable with the entire process."

The Four Eulogies: A vision exercise in which one chooses four people to speak at their funeral and one writes what they would want that person to say. What will people say about you at your death? (Page 50*)

The Four Rituals: The Morning Ritual, Pre-Leave Ritual, Nightly Ritual, and Sunday Night Ritual are proactive habits to help one become more efficient. (Pages 62–63,* 140)

FROG: An acronym to remember what to ask other people during phone calls and in-person meetings. F is for Family, R is for Recreation, O is for Occupation, and G is for Goals. (Pages 64,* 90)

The Generosity Generation: The Global Referral Community of the World's Most Referable Professionals. A new era of business where generous acts are rewarded. Givers are uniting to make a difference in the world. It is all about the consumer. It is about the "you". "It's all about relationships" is the slogan of the era. These businesses feed the soul. (Pages 13–15, 21, 27, 42, 126,* 129–130, 145, 153)

Geographic Farm: A group of people tied by location. Those who live in the same place. (Page 105*)

Google Alerts: Please go to alerts.google.com to learn more about Google Alerts. For the 7 Essential Google Alerts go to www.ReferralLibrary.com. (Page 15–16,* 118)

Gratitude Symbol: A charm, bracelet, or physical item that reminds one to be grateful.

The Great Re-Trace: Communicating with every person of a strand of referral sources. For example, Joe refers Jeff who introduced you to Cindy who recommended you to Janet. You would call Cindy with an update on Janet. Then you would call Jeff to express appreciation for connecting you to Cindy. Then you would call Joe to let him know what has happened. There is enormous, subtle power to this strategy. Learn more about Michael's legacy strategy, The Great Re-Trace Strategy, at www.ReferralLibrary.com. (Pages 135–136*)

The Guaranteed Response E-mail (GR@): An e-mail that invites people to call you. (Pages 118, 121, 122,* 126, 130)

Home Court Advantage: Becoming a regular at a local restaurant to create an "office away from the office". (Pages 64*–66)

The Hour of Power: An hour of focused outgoing phone calls to members of your Community. These are calls to your Community to see how you can help them. (Page 89*)

Impact Arrow: An arrow that depicts the impact, power, and effectiveness as you go up the Communication Pyramid. (Figures 2-1, 2-2, 2-3, 2-4, page 37*)

The Influential Zone: The top three levels of communication on the Communication Pyramid. Phone Calls, Events & Seminars, and One-on-One Meetings are the best way to influence, convince, or sell. The key to these levels is the element of feedback. You can listen and learn from the other person's tone and actions. (Figures 2-1, 2-2, 2-3, 2-4, pages 37,* 61, 78, 104)

Influencer: Person who has specific or universal credibility. Some people may have credibility within certain Communities – mayor of town or Membership Chair of city chamber. Some people may have nearly universal credibility – President of the United States, Mother Theresa, Billy Graham, some famous people.

The Informational Zone: The bottom three levels of communication on the Communication Pyramid. Advertising, Direct Mail, and Electronic Communication are terrific for informing, updating, and confirming. (Figures 2-1, 2-2, 2-3, 2-4, pages 37,* 116)

Key Questions: The two key questions that exemplify the philosophy of the Generosity Generation are "how can I help you" and "what can I do for you".

The Magic Question: "So that I may better serve you, please let me ask you a question. Out of the following four options – I'm going to give you four choices – how would your best friend or spouse BEST describe you. Would they describe you as 1) Straight-to-the-point, 2) Social & Outgoing, 3) Steady & Dependable, or 4) Cautious & Perfectly Accurate?" This question helps identify their DiSC behavioral style. (Pages 74,* 130)

Matching: Aligning your movement and pattern of speech to the other person. Author's Note: A One-on-One Meeting is a dance. There are the words and the music. You have to listen to the music and match your "rhythm" to the song your guest is singing. If your guest is "80s rock", you need to be "80s rock". You can see an example of this when one person tells the other of the loss of a loved one or a divorce. The one who hears the news instantly changes physically and their voice changes to match the other person.

Mirroring: 1) Repeating an affirmation back to the affirming person using the second-person (You). For example, Person1 says, "I am prepared and when I am prepared, I am unstoppable." Person2 mirrors back, "You ARE prepared and when you are prepared, you ARE unstoppable." 2) Mirroring the physical actions of another at a One-on-One Meeting.

The Morning Ritual: What one does from the moment the eyelids open to the time they arrive at work. With a morning ritual, one becomes more efficient, more positive, and more confident. Morning ritual components can include the following: reading, affirmations, mirroring with a partner, getting ready, exercising, dressing appropriately for the day, praying, listening to music, vision board review, and more. (Page 63*)

Net Promoter Score or Net Promoter System (NPS): A score based on a simple question to your Community—"How likely is it that you would recommend (company) to a friend or colleague?" The respondent answers on a 1 to 10 scale. Those who respond 9 or 10 are called Promoters. Those who response 7 or 8 are called Passives or Neutrals. Those who respond 6 or below are called Detractors. You calculate your NPS by subtracting the % of Detractors from the # of Promoters. For more read The Ultimate Question 2.0 by Fred Reichheld.

Networking Stack: Scheduling your networking appointments back-to-back to maximize your time. (Pages 63*–66, 151)

The Nightly Ritual: Pre-sleep routine including meditation, yoga, walking, reading, writing, and/or visualization of the next day. Studies have shown that adults and children who have pre-sleep routines sleep better. (Page 63*)

Peeling the Onion Phrases: "Tell me more about that" and "what is important about that to you" are the phrases that will allow one to find the underlying motivations for your client. (Page 90*)

The Perfect Work Day: Vision Exercise in which one goes hour-by-hour through their schedule imagining what would be perfect. (Pages 60–61*)

The Perfect Voicemail Greeting*: (Smile, record it like you are talking to your best friend!) "Thank you for calling the office of (your name). As always, you may press (skip digit) to skip this greeting at any time to leave your message. Again, you may press (skip digit) to skip this greeting. Because I want to provide you a level of service that makes it very easy and very comfortable for you to refer (whoever your target is) to me, I will be returning calls 11 am to Noon and 4 to 5 P.M. today so after the tone, please leave your name (1 sec), your number (1 sec), all the details and information you can provide so that I can better prepare myself to return your call (1 sec) and ALSO PLEASE leave the name of the person who referred my services to you so that I can get a prompt thank you out to them for that endorsement. Thank you for calling, have a great day, and remember, with (company name) (slogan)." *First heard about using greeting as more than a greeting from Joe Stumpf of By Referral Only® and in further research on DiSC® Behavioral Styles, telemarketing texts, and marketing books have changed it to current greeting. Feel free to adopt and adapt. (Page 50*)

POWER Note: The Ultimate Handwritten Note. Personal, Optimistic, Written, Effective, and Relational notes that build trust and get responses. (Pages 51,* 160)

The 7 Steps to a POWER Note (pages 51–52*):

1. Use unbranded, but representative cards
2. Use blue ink
3. Use the word "you" as much as possible and avoid words "I", "my", "me", and "we". You may use "we" when speaking in terms of the person you are writing and yourself, such as "we make a great team."
4. Be Specific with Praise
5. The Power of Positive Projection
6. Upwards and Onwards: Write Rightly.
7. The Plus of the P.S. in handwritten notes. Call-to-action.

Potential Champions ("B" Level Contact): Those who with more education and/or communication would refer you business. You just don't know if you are the one they would choose if someone had a need for your services. (Pages 103–105*)

The Pre-Leave Ritual: A time to get organized before leaving the office (even a home office). During the Pre-Leave Ritual, you organize the items on your desk, file, clean-up, trash, etc. your office. You will also write out/print out your 1st & 10 calls. (Page 63*)

Rainmaker: A businessperson who creates a large amount of unexpected business, consistently brings in money at critical times, or brings in markedly more money than his or her co-workers, thereby "floating their salaries". An executive, lawyer, or business owner with exceptional ability to attract clients, use political connections, or increase profits, etc. (Pages 50, 151)

Rainmaker's Affirmation: Each and every day, someone, somewhere in my city needs my services. My job TODAY is to find that person. (Page 50*)

Referral script—basic: "Who is the next person you know who will be buying, selling, or investing in real estate?" or "Who do you know who will be buying, selling, or investing in real estate?" (Page 92)

Referral script—"Great people": "That's great. You know, something I've found in my business is that great people tend to know other great people. So with that in mind, out of all the people you know, who is the next person who will be buying, selling, or investing in real estate?" (Page 92)

Referral script—Who-like-you: "Who is another first time home buyer like you who will be looking for homes soon?" and/or "Who else do you know who will be (buying, selling, investing, moving, looking, relocating, etc.)?" (Page 92)

Reticular Activating System (RAS): Functions of the reticular activating system are many and varied. Among other functions, it contributes to the control of sleep, walking, sex, eating, and elimination. Perhaps the most important function of the RAS is its control of consciousness. It is believed to control sleep, wakefulness, and the ability to consciously focus attention on something. In addition, the RAS acts as a filter, dampening down the effect of repeated stimuli such as loud noises, helping to prevent the senses from being overloaded. You can invoke other's RAS by reminding them and letting them know situations when this memory may occur. (Page 93)

Solutions: The reason people come to you and pay for your services. (Page 79)

Spectrum of Solutions: A document depicting and listing the solutions provided by a company, salesperson, or owner. For samples of Spectrums of Solutions, please go to www.ReferralLibrary. com. (Page 79*)

Spokes-to-Hubs Strategy: This strategy utilizes who you know to meet someone you don't know. You think about those who are most likely to know the Hub. Those you know can connect you (Spokes) to the (Hub). You simply ask if they will introduce or call that person on your behalf. With several or more doing this, the person responds to your inquiry. Coaching clients have done this with Asset Managers, HR Executives, Property Managers, Developers, Active Adult Community Managers, etc. (Page 94*)

The Success Series: A series of informative communication pieces (Success Stories) scheduled at regular times to go to one's Community. (Page 109*)

Success Story: A narrative about one of your clients. The Swiss Army Knife of communication. (Pages 68,* 119, 130, 145)

The 7 Steps to a Successful Success Story. (Page 68*)
1. Who was the client and what was their category? (1st timer, repeat client, investor, executive, etc.)
2. What is the WORST-CASE SCENARIO for this client category? (Think NUCLEAR CASE here.)
3. How did you help them solve the problem?
4. What was the result? Be specific.
5. What did the client say or do to let you know you did well?
6. Ask for SPECIFIC and RELEVANT Referrals
7. Call to Action.

Success Suicide: The act of self-sabotage that occurs when an old self-image is being replaced with a new and better self-image. Also called the breakdown before the breakthrough this is a self-imposed barrier that blocks people from the next level of success. (Pages 53,* 85)

The Sunday Night Ritual: Weekly ritual to review the coming days. This ritual includes such things as laying out/hanging up outfits for each day of the week to match weather and events of the day. Menu planning for the week is suggested. The questions of "what am I going to wear?" and "what am I going to eat?" are answered proactively so that besides saving you valuable time and decreasing stress, you look and feel like a million bucks. (Page 63*)

Thermometer or 1 to 10 script: Used to determine motivation or degree. Used with 1 being the lowest level and 10 being the highest level. For example, on a scale of 1 to 10 with 1 being you are just curious and 10 being you need to buy a home today, where do you find yourself on that scale? A. 5. Great! A 5. What would it take to make that a 10? A. I need to get pre-approved. 1 to 10 script can be used in a multitude of situations. (Pages 44, 95)

Time Blocking: Scheduling proactive, standard, and general appointments within your calendar (some block off down to 15-minute, 30-minute, and/or 1-hour increments). (Pages 61*–62, 144)

Triangle of Trust: Simple concept that depicts the introduction of two trusted individuals to each other. Josh knows, likes, and trusts Rick. Josh knows, likes, and trusts Michelle. Michelle asks Josh to introduce her to Rick. When Michelle and Rick meet, they begin to form the third side of the Triangle of Trust. There is already a dotted line formed because Rick and Michelle are borrowing on Josh's trust. Concept is integral to the strategy that rather than marketing to strangers, a business can grow quickly and profitably by communicating with those people they know (current clients, key contacts, and referral partners). There is tremendous power to this concept. (Pages 93–94, 95*–98)

The Ultimate Client Experience: A vision exercise taking the A to Z client system to the point of visualization and making large impact at every moment of truth—every piece of communication with the client. Imagining, documenting, and improving the process flow through your orgnanization's transactional timeline through the eyes of the client. Every element, mode, medium, and piece of communication is analyzed either by clients or through the eyes of the client.

The Ultimate Memory Jogger: A document that helps you to think of everyone you know. It simply jogs your memory to remember those you've met, been connected to, or been associated with over the years. Visit www.ReferralLibrary.com/ultimate memoryjogger for more. (Pages 105,* 144)

VIP Form: Questionnaire for new members of your Community. Helps you get to know the person better, drops hint about referrals, and helps you build rapport. For examples of VIP Forms, please go to www.ReferralLibrary.com/vip for more.

HEARTFELT APPRECIATION

IT WOULD BE IMPOSSIBLE to acknowledge all those who have had an impact on me during my life.

I am grateful to God for His plan for me and Jesus for the role model He provides me personally and professionally.

It all starts with my wife, Sheri, and my son, Max. They support me and inspire me on a daily basis. This book is dedicated to my father, Patrick J. Maher. My mother, Mary Ann Maher, is one of the smartest people I've ever known and raised five great children while excelling at work. My siblings—Steve, Susan, Brian, and Rob—mean the world to me and were instrumental in helping me become who I am.

There are teachers who appeared when the student—me—was ready. Howard Brinton, Larry Kendall, Joe Stumpf, Brian Buffini, Floyd Wickman and Allen Hainge are leaders of organizations that have had a major impact on my life.

I'd like to acknowledge the By Referral Only®, Star Power Star® and CyberStar® families. It is an honor and privilege to be a part of these families.

Authors and other influential people who have made a major impact on me are as follows: Bob Burg, Dr. Ivan Misner, Dr. Tony Alessandra, Bob Corcoran, Zig Ziglar, Jim Rohn, John C. Maxwell, John David Mann, Tony Robbins, Jim Collins, Marcus Buckingham, Seth Godin, Tim Templeton, Regis McKenna, Jeffrey Gitomer, Dr. Stephen R. Covey, Harvey Mackay, Gary Keller, Dave Jenks, Jay Papasan, Tom Hopkins, Brian Tracy, Gary Vaynerchuk, Ken Blanchard, Spencer Johnson, Jack Canfield, Mark Victor Hansen, Matthey Kelly, Joe Pine, Jim Gilmore, Jon Gordon, Dr. Robert Cialdini, Kevin Hogan, Jay Conrad Levinson, Danielle Kennedy, Tom Ferry and Loral Langemeier.

Others who deserve special mention are the following: Dave Ramsey, Barry Habib, Todd Duncan, Dave Savage, Tim Braheem, Richard Robbins, David Knox, Rick DeLuca, Greg Frost, Tim Davis, Jay Kinder, Erik Janeczko, Stephanie York, Cleve Adams, Cantey Tull and Gary Ogami.

I have to express my utmost appreciation for this book's Board of Advisors. In alphabetical order, they are Dan Auito, Brian Copeland, Seth & Alyce Dailey, Tammy Ebright, Stephanie Evelo, Larry Goodell, Brad Korn, Jonas Kruckeberg, Chris Lundine, Aaron Magruder, Maura Neill, James Nellis, Jacob Nordby, Mike Parker, C. Spencer Reynolds, Christian Russell, Amy Stoehr, David Van Noy, Jr., Jason W. Womack and Mark Zervos.

Lastly, I appreciate you. Thank you for investing in (7L). I've poured my heart and soul into this book wanting to provide as much value as possible for your investment. Also, please know that a portion of every book sale goes to charity. Thank you.

MICHAEL J. MAHER

Michael J. Maher is one of North America's most dynamic, thought-provoking, and energizing professional speakers. Each year, he travels more than 100,000 miles delivering his powerful wisdom on leadership, mastery, productivity, and life management to major corporations, chambers, associations, real estate professionals, mortgage professionals, financial advisors, insurance agents, entrepreneurs, and small business owners. His customized conference keynotes and in-house seminars are in constant demand by organizations seeking an educational and entertaining professional speaker who will provide immediately effective strategies to help their people reach all-new levels of productivity, performance, and personal satisfaction.

Michael J. Maher's current programs include:

✓ *Secrets of the Most Referred Professionals in the World*
✓ *Go from Relationships to Referrals Without Asking for Referrals*
✓ *The 3.5 Most Powerful Referral-Generating Questions of All Time*
✓ *Go from Relationships to Referrals Using Social Media*
✓ *Winning in Business in the Generosity Generation*
✓ *The 7 Things That Matter Most (to Your Professional Success)*
✓ *THE FIX: Go from Chaos to Clarity and Solve Overwhelm Forever*

All programs are customized to maximize attendees' experience: audience, theme of event, and incorporating host.

For a complete listing of Michael's programs, products, high-profile clients, and speaking schedule, visit his website at www.MichaelJMaher.com.

To book Michael J. Maher for your next conference or in-house event, please contact*:
Director of Live Experiences
Toll-Free: 1-800-752-4363

*For best and fastest response, please fill out Speaking Request Form at www.MichaelJMaher.com.